The Gallows Tree

Crime and Punishment in the 18th Century

~

Northumberland and Berwick-upon-Tweed

Barry Redfern

Tyne Bridge Publishing

Acknowledgements

My sincere thanks are offered to the following for access to books and papers. The staff at the Public Record Office, the Chief Archivists and Librarians at Tyne and Wear Archives, Northumberland Record Office, City Library, Newcastle upon Tyne and also Morpeth and Berwick; the Hall family at the Raw; R. Trevelyan Esq. Netherwitton Hall; John Brown Esq of Knowesgate; Anna Flowers, Vanessa Histon and the team at Tyne Bridge Publishing and finally to my family and friends who have encouraged and supported my research for the past 25 years.

Barry Redfern, Newcastle upon Tyne, 2013

Unless otherwise indicated, illustrations are from collections at Newcastle Libraries.

The Gallows Tree is a companion to *The Shadow of the Gallows: Crime and Punishment on Tyneside in the Eighteenth Century* by Barry Redfern (2003). This book is out of print but a free downloadable copy can be found at www.newcastle.gov.uk/libraries or at www.tynebridgepublishing.co.uk

Also by Barry Redfern: *Victorian Villains: Prisoners from Newcastle Gaol 1871-1873* (Tyne Bridge Publishing, 2006, £6.99), case studies and fascinating accounts of crime and punishment from Newcastle's earliest police photographic records.

©Barry Redfern, 2013
Published by
City of Newcastle upon Tyne
Newcastle Libraries & Information Service
Tyne Bridge Publishing, 2013

www.tynebridgepublishing.co.uk
www.newcastle.gov.uk/libraries

ISBN: 978-1-85795-213-1

Printed by Martins the Printers, Berwick-upon-Tweed

Contents

Introduction

The Gallows Tree is a companion to *The Shadow of the Gallows* (Tyne Bridge Publishing, October 2003; out of print, but see page 2 for downloadable e-book edition) and extends the account of crime and punishment in the 18th century beyond Newcastle to Northumberland and Berwick-upon-Tweed. Criminal justice in Northumberland and Newcastle upon Tyne were interlocked in many ways. The general focus is on the 18th century but occasionally we start earlier or end later to complete the accounts of some of the institutions and other matters.

The justices of Northumberland had problems of delays and distance to deal with, in contrast to their friends and colleagues on the bench at Newcastle upon Tyne. As will be seen in some of the stories, criminals active in Northumberland could quickly escape into the borders. The remote nature of parts of Northumberland perhaps gave these villains the self confidence to expect they could evade capture. However, the 18th century Northumbrian parish constables and justices were a hardy breed of men possessed of common sense and much determination to seek out the robbers and housebreakers of their day. They operated under difficult conditions but they resolutely set about pursuing criminals and, as was the custom of the time, bringing them to the gallows or the holds of the convict ships crossing the Atlantic Ocean, for the greater part of that century.

Berwick-upon-Tweed has a unique history of isolation and the justices conducted their trials of serious crimes without the benefit of high court judges. They were tied into the legal profession of Northumberland and Newcastle upon Tyne in other ways. Eventually, in the 19th century, Berwick-upon-Tweed was drawn fully into the legal circuits. Anyone wishing to know more about the 18th century life of Berwick-upon-Tweed is urged to read that first class study of the subject by David Brenchley, *A Place by Itself* (Berwick-upon-Tweed Civic Society, 1997).

The Gallows Tree and *The Shadow of the Gallows* are based on legal records and many other contemporary sources, of necessity much summarised here. More detailed information is available in the Heritage Section, City Library, Newcastle upon Tyne.

Barry Redfern, Newcastle upon Tyne, 2013

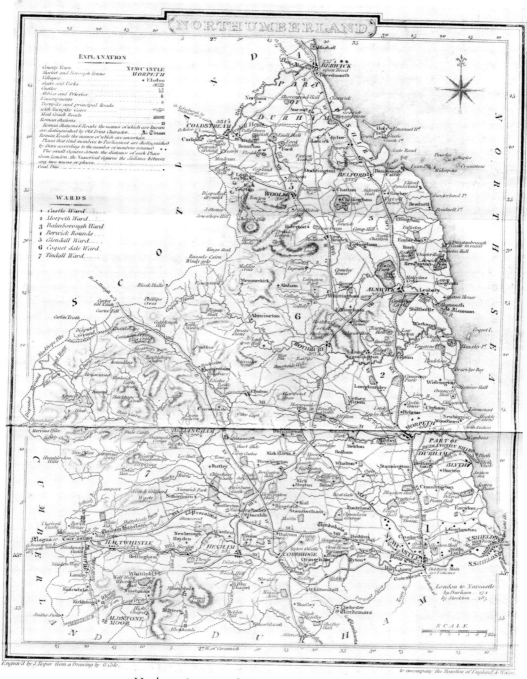

Hodgson's map of Northumberland, 1818.

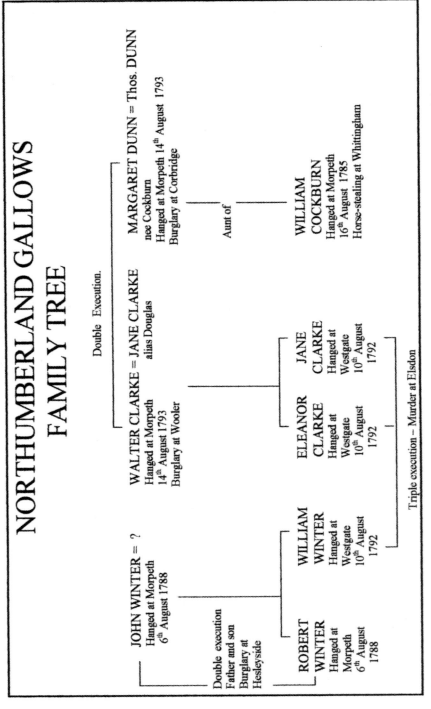

NORTHUMBERLAND GALLOWS FAMILY TREE

Double Execution.

JOHN WINTER = ?
Hanged at Morpeth
6th August 1788

WALTER CLARKE = JANE CLARKE
alias Douglas
Hanged at Morpeth
14th August 1793
Burglary at Wooler

MARGARET DUNN = Thos. DUNN
nee Cockburn
Hanged at Morpeth 14th August 1793
Burglary at Corbridge

Aunt of

Double execution
Father and son
Burglary at
Hesleyside

ROBERT WINTER
Hanged at
Morpeth
6th August
1788

WILLIAM WINTER
Hanged at
Westgate
10th August
1792

ELEANOR CLARKE
Hanged at
Westgate
10th August
1792

JANE CLARKE
Hanged at
Westgate
10th August
1792

WILLIAM COCKBURN
Hanged at Morpeth
16th August 1785
Horse-stealing at Whittingham

Triple execution – Murder at Elsdon

The 'gallows family tree' shows the close relationship between the notorious Winter family and members of the Faws gangs.

1. Hangman's Land

> **The Burgesses and community of Morpeth, by deed without date, demised to Patrick the hangman of Morpeth, a rood of land, out of which the bridge and chapel there had an annual rent of 4s. 0d. (Annals, 1307 No. 4)**
>
> They also let it again in 1326 and Hangman's Land is mentioned in 1463 and 1465.
>
> (*A History of Morpeth* by John Hodgson, 1832 Page 75)

This reference to an executioner of 1307, found by John Hodgson, seems to be all that is known about Patrick the Hangman of Morpeth, but it serves to highlight the profusion of place names in Northumberland associated with the gallows. Long before the 18th century, each of the shire counties and county boroughs entitled to have their own sitting of the Assize Court had to have a place to put up a gallows if a permanent gallows was not already in place. Northumberland had two gallows sites, the first was at Fair Moor on the north side of Morpeth and the other was outside the West Gate in the town walls of Newcastle upon Tyne.

Trawling through the county histories and other sources produces an extraordinary cache of ancient gallows place names scattered about the county.

Hangman's Hill on Acomb Fell.
Gallow Law Camp and *Gallow Law Field* at Alwinton.
Gallowburn Plantation on the Middleton estate at Belsay.
Gallows Hill at Bolam.
Gallowhill, *Gallow Hill Balk*, *Gallow Holme* and *Bloody Acre*, field names on the banks of the River Tyne east of Corbridge.
Gallows Hill on the hill north of Corbridge.

Gallows Hill south of Elsdon.

Gallows Side at Haltwhistle

Gallow Law and *Gallow Edge* at Harbottle.

Gallow Hill and *Gallows Close* at Harbourne.

Gallow Hill at Hartington.

Gallow Law north of Low Hedgeley.

Gallows Close, a field name at Hepple.

Hangman's Acre, on level land between Hexham and the River Tyne.

Hangman's Wood, overlooking Hexham on the hill south of the town.

Gallowshaw, a farm at Netherwitton.

Gallow Moor near Rock.

Gallowfield between Rothbury and Thropton.

Gallow Hill near the Roman Wall above Thirlwall Castle.

Why do so many Northumbrian place names relate to gallows? There is a link to the number of castles in the county, as explained in John Hodgson's *History of Northumberland* published in 1827:

> **Prior to the Norman Conquest, and for a long time after, the barons of the greater part of Europe were nearly absolute lords in their own domains [and] were under little control by their kings.**

The barons of Northumberland claimed the right of judging and hanging thieves within their manors. Hodgson goes on to discuss the problems of the borders and the obstinacy of the 'Redesdale and Tindale men' clinging to the ways and privileges of Saxon times. Gilbert de Umfreville, Earl of Angus c1239-c1307, claimed the right of gallows at Prudhoe Castle, Harbottle, Redesdale, 'Alwenton' and elsewhere. His right to have a gaol at Harbottle was granted in 1336; and confirmed in 1361. He was given permission to keep prisoners in his prison of Prudhoe Castle until Harbottle Castle, ruined by wars with the Scots, was repaired. Going back to 1294, Gilbert De Umfreville claimed the right of a gallows, tumbrel (a form of ducking stool), pillory and tolls at Elsdon.

Early records survive to link the gallows place names around Corbridge to the claim by Robert Fitz Roger to the right of gallows in his manor. In 1293, Ralph, a servant of Hugh de Burton of Corbridge, was hanged for stealing goods worth 20 marks by burglary at his master's house. William 'son of David of Scotland' was hanged for the same offence. Other accomplices were outlawed and one, who was a chaplain, was handed over to the Bishop and eventually died in the Bishop's prison. In another example that year 'Richard the Miller of Corbridge and Thomas Onyon his brother and Catelina their mother' were hanged at Corbridge for stealing meat from Richard de Heryngton (*History of Northumberland*, Northumberland History Committee 1914, page 72). Whether these people were hanged on Gallows Hill at Corbridge or in one of the fields next to the River Tyne, bearing gallows names is open to speculation.

So, part of the impact of local law enforcement by the barons of Northumberland within their own lands was the growth of place names associated with their power to hang felons, and the names endure to this day.

The list above is unlikely to be complete. On the back page of the *Newcastle Courant* for Saturday 29 September 1753 is an advertisement for the sale of Gallowhill, Northumberland. 'The real estate of Mark Aynsley late of Gallowhill in Northumberland, deceased, lying in the parishes of Bolam and Morpeth, three lots – High Gallowhill, Low Gallowhill and Fowmertlaw. High Gallowhill includes the mansion house.'

The 18th century residents of Northumberland probably took the place names for granted; capital punishment was a fact of life.

Prudhoe Castle around 1780.

2. Enforcing the Law

> We hear if any of the prosecutors, in the County of Northumberland, shall neglect to carry in their bills before the Grand Jury, immediately after the charge is given on Monday morning next, that in such case, they will not be allowed any thing out of the county stock.
>
> *Newcastle Courant* Saturday 7 August, 1773

This warning to prosecutors probably came from the county justices and serves to highlight the huge difference between enforcing the criminal law in Northumberland and the rest of the country in the 18th century and in the present day. It was all down to the individual – the victim, or his relatives and friends in the case of a murder – to make something happen. There were no police forces or public prosecution bodies to pursue felons and bring them to justice. If the victim failed to follow through at the Quarter Sessions or Assizes their prosecution did not even reach the starting post of an 18th century race to a verdict, consideration by the Grand Jury.

Unfortunately it is not clear whether this warning that reluctant prosecutors would not receive any financial support from the county worked or not. The following *Newcastle Courant* account of results at the Northumberland Assizes the following week did not report any failures to prosecute, although the Grand Jury did not find sufficient evidence to pursue trials against four people. But were John Wompray, or any of others, discharged because the victim did not appear at the trial or simply found not guilty? Four convictions out of 16 prosecutions do not encourage confidence in the system.

At the same time [i.e. Thursday 12th] ended the Assizes for the County of Northumberland, when William Orr for robbery, received sentence of death. Joseph Sproat for stealing a watch, to be transported for seven years, John Harper for stealing a silver can burnt in the hand, and sent to the house of correction for 3 months, Alexander Frazier for house-breaking sent to the house of correction for a week, and to be whipt through Morpeth next Market Day, John Wompray, Robert Davison, Robert Allen, John Stewart, Ann Wilson, Jane Taylor, Elizabeth Lark and John Bouser were discharged. Robert Davison, Thomas Forest, Edward Harvey and John Mude, no indictments were found against them.

(Note: William Orr was later reprieved for transportation, Davison and Forest were held for murder, Harvey and Mude for arson.)

Newcastle Courant Saturday 14 August, 1773

This simple illustration reveals some of the problems and difficulties of the time. The backdrop to the drama of crime, chase, trial, executions and so on, is a large shire county of beaches, fertile plains and hills, emerging from centuries of border troubles and civil strife. It was a land of market towns, fishing ports, and many remote and vulnerable villages and hamlets. Communities were facing up to change as people were drawn to Tyneside by the growing industrial activity resting on the wealth of the coalfields. The growth of the urban districts then, as today, brought with it anonymity for the criminal fraternity and increasing crime. Only the smaller communities retained that close and personal knowledge of local people who could spot the wrong-doer in their midst and, as the first layer in the 18th century justice system, make enforcing the law work effectively.

There are many tales of courageous Northumbrians standing up for themselves when attacked on the highways – none better than that of Adam Bird of North Shields in 1742:

On Saturday night [ie.16th Oct. 1742] Mr Adam Bird, of North Shields, returning home from this Place, was attack'd on the Road, about two Miles out of Town, by a Person on Foot, who, seizing hold of his Horse's Bridle, and at the same time presenting a Pistol to his Breast, demanded his Money. Mr Bird, not startled in the least at this unexpected and strange Salute, ask'd him If he was in earnest? The Villain answer'd, with a G----d d-----n his B---d! he was; and if he did not immediately deliver, he'd blow his brains out. He had no sooner got the Words out of his Mouth, than Mr Bird gave him so hearty a Stroke over the Head with But-end of his Whip, that it knock'd him down. Here a sad Misfortune had like to have Happened, for in the Fall the Pistol went off; but it providentially did no Execution, the Ball only grazing his Ear. Mr Bird hereupon dismounted; but, being lame of one of his Feet, occasioned by an Anchor of 15 or 16 Ct. Wt falling on it only the Week before, was not quick enough to secure the Rogue, who having recover'd himself, had got over the Hedge into the Fields, and escap'd.

Newcastle Courant, Saturday 23 October 1742

The spirit of the Hue and Cry still prevailed. The stories told elsewhere in this book illustrate how this worked in practice in the 18th century. When the victim of a crime called for help, then those around him were required to assist in whatever way they could to capture the thief and recover property. But a victim could find himself involved in costs and expenses pursuing a criminal, offering rewards, for example, and advertising. There were exceptions in special circumstances as will be seen in the chapter about the Faw Gangs. These people were seen as such a threat to the county at large that the justices offered special rewards for their capture several times during the century. Also in the story that lies behind the famous landmark 'Winter's Gibbet', the elders of Elsdon Parish offered payment of a reward for the arrest of those responsible for the murder of Margaret Crozier.

No formal records were required to be kept about reports of crime so, except for one brief list mentioned below, 18th century crime statistics for Northumberland have not survived. Some commentators take the view that crime was generally increasing in the country during the 18th century but on the other hand it is said that the North East was no better or worse than elsewhere.

Something significant happened during the 18th century. Groups of potential victims around the country, trades people in a town or city for example, would come together and form an 'Association for the Prosecution of Felons'. This was a form of self-help group aimed at providing support, particularly financial, in the process through to prosecution and trial, when one of their members became a victim of crime. It is an indicator of fear of crime, difficulties with the current system and even lack of confidence in the process of enforcing the law. Members of these associations were people of standing in the community, perhaps justices of the peace and certainly potential jurors, so conflicts of interest could easily arise. On the plus side, however, the financial clout of associations supported prosecutions and helped to ensure criminals were brought to trial.

If the first level of the system for dealing with crime in country districts was the victim and those immediately around him, the second level was the parish or petty constable. This parish official was appointed annually. He was unpaid, except for expenses, and probably reluctant to take the office because he had his own work to do, whatever that might be. He would be supplied with a decorated truncheon as a symbol of authority and sometimes handcuffs, but he would receive no training and would be expected to learn by experience. His many duties, in addition to enforcing the criminal law, included inspecting ale houses, collecting rates and taxes, controlling beggars, vagabonds and pauper children, and support work for the coroner. He also administered the stocks, pillory and ducking stool. But it is the parish constable as a link between the victim and the justice of the peace that is of special interest here. If the victim and helpers had secured the thief, the constable took charge of the prisoner and, assisted by the victim and others as required, took the prisoner before a justice for committal to gaol. In the *Curry's Point* chapter a variation of this occurs where the son of the murder victim accompanied the constable to North Shields to arrest the suspect, Michael Curry. Turning to the chapter about *Winter's Gibbet*, the whole of a remote parish community came together to seek out those responsible for the dreadful murder of Margaret Crozier.

Generally speaking, there were regular examples of parish constables working effectively and with determination. However, there must also have been some uneven quality or standards amongst the petty constables of Northumberland leading to a complaint and warning from the justices in 1772. They pointed out that many of the county's communities were so small that it would be difficult for offenders to hide for long if the constables were doing their jobs properly. They threatened:

> **that inflicting punishment upon a few constables or other peace officers, for misbehaviour in their office, would be of more real advantage to the county, for example's sake than punishing double the number of common offenders.**
>
> *Newcastle Courant* 21 November 1772

Each hundred had a public official called a high constable, usually a gentleman, who appears to have overseen the work of petty constables, in connection with forming juries for example. He received reports from the constables, but played no part in crime investigations.

In Northumberland in the early part of the 18th century there was a force still at work from earlier times called 'country keepers.' The system is described in some detail by Hodgson Hinde (*History of Northumberland* 1858 p.392-394). The force was developed in the 17th century during the border troubles to deal with the intrusions by moss troopers (border thieves). It was funded by a 'country-keeping cess,' a tax levied on the land and property owners of Northumberland, and had a duty to protect vulnerable people from thefts by the moss troopers. The Country Keeper, i.e. the head or leader of the force, was appointed by the justices at their sessions and was usually a gentleman of the county. The keeper was paid a salary of around £500 a year to provide and run the force. An act of 1662 authorised the appointment of a keeper and not more than 30 men for Northumberland. There was a requirement for compensation to be paid for stolen goods that were not recovered. For example in the records of the Michaelmass Sessions in 1713 there is a long list of crimes in Northumberland for which compensation was paid, including 123 reports of the theft of live-stock, sheep, cattle and horses, valued at £303 1s. 6d. (Northumberland Record Office Access No. QSO5.) Such an arrangement was open to abuse by false claims and among the many references to country keepers in the sessions' records there are protests from the justices about malpractice. The justices laid out formal arrangements for posting details of crimes and requirements for formal proof before compensation would be paid. (Christmas Sessions 1721/2 and Midsummer Sessions 1726. Northumberland Record Office Access No. QSO 6.) Hodgson Hinde makes it clear that the force did not have a credible public image but it continued to operate long past the time when the moss troopers had ceased to be a major problem. References in county records to the country keepers peter out in the middle of the 18th century.

The next layer in the enforcement process were the justices of the peace, a post usually held by country gentlemen, the squires of the parishes. Sitting together as the 'Quarter Sessions of the Peace', they dealt with a wide range of matters, not just crime, and were effectively the government of the county. Technically speaking, they administered many things that were the ultimate responsibility of the High Sheriff (see below). Their responsibilities were quite different from those of modern magistrates. The four venues for the 18th century county sessions were the Moot Hall at Newcastle upon Tyne, the Moot Hall at Hexham, the Town Hall at Morpeth and Town Hall at Alnwick. But when dealing with the day-to-day crime problems of the countryside, the county justice did not sit in a court and, as the following examples illustrate, it was common for the parish constable to bring prisoners to the home of the justice for him to consider committal to the county gaol.

The justice began a more detailed enquiry. Assisted by the constable he interviewed witnesses, setting down written sworn evidence in what are called depositions. The justice also 'examined' the prisoners, taking evidence of their explanations or confessions. The justice played a positive and active role in the law enforcement process. A good example is Walter Trevelyan of Netherwitton, the justice in the Winter's Gibbet case. He was tireless in his pursuit of county criminals and his name crops up at regular intervals in the 18th century newspapers and county records. The depositions taken by the justices were passed to the Clerk of the Peace for the county to prepare the charges, known as indictments, against the prisoners.

Appointed annually by the crown and at the top of this law enforcement pyramid was the High Sheriff of Northumberland. All the senior gentlemen of the county were expected and required to take on this heavy task and become the King's representative for a year. In 1786, John Impey of the Inner Temple summed up the sheriff's general responsibilities for controlling crime:

As the keeper of the king's peace both by common and special commission, he is the first man in the county, and superior in rank to any nobleman therein, during his office (I Roll Rep 237). He may apprehend, and commit to prison, all persons who break the peace, or attempt to break; and may bind anyone to keep the king's peace. He may, and is bound ex offcio to pursue, and take all traitors, murderers, felons and other misdoers, and commit them to gaol for safe custody. He is also to defend his county against all the king's enemies when they come into the land. And for the purpose, as well as for keeping the peace, and pursuing felons, he may command all the people of his county to attend him; which is called posse comitatus or power of the county.

The Office of Sheriff shewing its History and Antiquity by John Impey of the Inner Temple, published London 1786 Page 53 (Northumberland Record Office NRO 542/1) (Note 'all persons' above meant everyone over 15 years of age.)

The sheriff was also responsible for the gaols and gaolers. Much of the day-to-day administration of these tasks was, as outlined earlier, delegated to justices individually or jointly at the Quarter Sessions, but strictly speaking the sheriff carried the final responsibility. It was an onerous task and an expensive one. Not everyone wanted to accept the post but there were financial penalties for failing to do so and it was also discourteous to the King. Sir Lancelot Allgood of Nunwick was the High Sheriff of Northumberland at the time of the rebellion of 1745 and his expenses for that year in office are recorded in the family papers as £1,000, a huge sum by today's standards (Northumberland CRO ZAL 98/8/2).

The temporary status of the sheriff as 'the first man in the county,' is very clearly shown in the annual procession to meet the judges of assize. Up to 300 horsemen and perhaps 30 coaches set out from the Moot Hall about the beginning of August each year and passed up Sheriff Hill in Gateshead led by the High Sheriff in a fine coach. Normally he may have been outranked by some of the gentlemen in the procession. By a strange twist of ancient protocol, though, the High Sheriff was required to sit with his back to the horses on the return journey back to Newcastle upon Tyne with the judges.

The stage was set for the next stage in the process, trial by the high court judges. The Northumberland Assizes were held in the old Moot Hall, at Castlegarth, Newcastle upon Tyne, which was demolished in 1810. First, there was a pre-trial procedure, a review of the evidence for each case by the Grand Jury. The list of 24 men for the Grand Jury was like a roll call of the titled and landed gentry of Northumberland.

> The following gentlemen composed the Grand Jury for the County of Northumberland: Sir Walter Blackett Bart., Foreman, Sir Matthew White Ridley, Bart., the Hon Sir Francis Blake Delaval Knight of the Bath, Sir Lancelot Allgood, Knt., Sir Robert Bewick, Knt., George Delaval, Matthew Ridley, Edward Collingwood, William Ord, Christopher Reed, William Carr, Henry Collingwood, Matthew Forster, Henry Ellison, Bryan Burrell, Percival Clennell, Henry Hudson, Ralph Bates, George Craister, Aubone Surtees, John Simpson, John Ord, and Gabriel Selby, Esqrs.
>
> *Newcastle Journal* Saturday 22 August 1767

The foreman took a special oath before presiding over the deliberations of the Grand Jury.

The work of the Grand Jury might be described as an exercise in quality control to ensure that indictments supported by credible evidence were passed forward for a full trial before the judge and a petit jury of 12 men.

The week when the judges came to town was known as Assize Week, a time of much pageantry and excitement in Newcastle upon Tyne, in contrast to the grim business of the trials where a person's life would rest on the scales of justice. The trials, decisions and punishments awarded by the judges at the assizes and the justices at the sessions will be discussed in a later chapter. But, here to round off this description of law enforcement in the 18th century, are the views of a man with a long and special experience of crime in Northumberland. When Frederic Hill (the first inspector for the North East) paid his first visit to Morpeth Gaol in February 1838 he asked John Blake, the long serving gaoler, for his view of the state of crime in Northumberland. These were John Blake's recollections and opinions based upon 50 years' experience in charge of the county gaol.

Mr. Blake states that there has not been much crime in the county of late years, and that there is considerably less than there was when he was young; that the most common offences at the present time are thefts (unaccompanied by violence) and poaching, with assaults and other offences arising therefrom. Fifty years ago, however, Mr. Blake says, that murder was not uncommon: and that there was a good deal of highway robbery, housebreaking, horse-stealing and sheep-stealing; while smuggling, with its attendant offences, was of constant occurrence. At that time executions were common. Mr. Blake remembers six in one year (1792), whereas 16 years have now passed without a single execution, and at the same time, many fewer offences are committed with impunity now rather than formerly. Indeed, it is Mr. Blake's belief that during the whole of the last 16 years only one deliberate murder has been committed and that was in the case of a new born infant. He believes, also, that there has been no bad case of highway robbery during the same period. When he was a young man Mr. Blake says, there was a formidable gang of robbers, many of them gypsies, whom farmers were afraid to prosecute. Now, however, there are no such gangs nor any other organised system of robbery.

Mr. Blake's experience confirms what I have often remarked, that crime runs to a considerable extent in families.

(3rd Report of the Inspectors Appointed to Visit the Different Prisons of Great Britain, 1838)

3. Curry's Point

The Northumberland coastal village of Hartley stands in the parish of Earsdon, a mile or two north of Whitley Bay. For centuries the people there relied on salt, the sea and coal for their livelihood. The 17th and 18th century parish church registers have survived and they contain an abundance of births, marriages and burials for the family names of Raw, Chater and Shevill of Hartley in a great variety of spellings as was the custom of the time.

When Isabel Chater married a mariner, Thomas Raw, at Earsdon Parish Church on Christmas Day 1727, little did she know that the next 15 years or so would bring one tragedy after another into her life. Isabel Chater/Raw was then 27 years of age; she had four children to Thomas Raw, all of whom died in infancy, the eldest at just five years. On 19 January 1734/5 she buried her fourth child, John, aged four months at Earsdon churchyard and eight days later, on 27 January 1734/5, she was back at the church for the funeral of her husband Thomas Raw.

On 18 September 1737 Isabel Raw married another local man, Robert Shevill, who was a colliery overman and also kept one of the three inns serving the small village, The Three Horseshoes, Hartley. The couple had one daughter named Isabel after her mother, but this child was only seven-and-a-half years old when she died. However before that happened the

A view of Hartley around 1914, 150 years after the Curry's Point murder.

father, Robert Shevill, was murdered by his wife's lover and Isabel Shevill was charged with complicity in the crime.

Sometime before December 1738 Robert Shevill took in a lodger at the Three Horseshoes Inn at 3s 6d per week. His name was Michael Curry; his age is not known but his trade was said to be a 'Sinker of Coal Pitts', which probably meant he was one of those men who excavated and opened up the numerous bell pits in the North East to reach the coal seams at shallow depth. Curry was the son of Ralph Curry of Low Lights at North Shields, where there were navigation lights to help mariners line up on the safe route for ships when entering the River Tyne.

Robert Shevill discovered Curry naked in Mrs Shevill's bedroom on 7 December 1738. He described what happened in a sworn statement on 6 January. When Shevill asked Curry what he was doing, Curry replied that he wanted a drink of water. Shevill pointed out that the water was downstairs and said he suspected that Curry had visited Isabel's bedchamber more than once. He gave Curry one week's notice to quit his lodging, but Isabel said Curry could stay whether her husband agreed or not.

Seven days notice to quit the inn seems remarkably generous in the circumstances but the fact that Shevill later went to the trouble of making a sworn deposition about the incident and that his wife was prepared to defy him suggests that he was deeply afraid of Curry and concerned about the future. Such fear was well founded and two days after making that deposition Shevill was still not entirely rid of Michael Curry. Curry's father, Ralph, later described visiting the Three Horseshoes on 8 January and eating and drinking in the company of his son Michael, Isabel Shevill and William and Thomas Lawson, who were half-brothers of Mrs Shevill. Ralph Curry asked Mrs Shevill where her husband was and she said, 'he had taken the pett.' Michael was said to have slept that night at a house in Earsdon, but his father spent the night at the Three Horseshoes. The following day Robert Shevill walked with Ralph Curry on part of his journey to North Shields. Before parting Shevill told him that 'he wanted to be quitt of his son Michael Curry.'

The final and fatal encounter between the two men took place in the early hours of Thursday 11 January 1738/39. Michael Curry somehow gained access to the Three Horseshoes, which was locked and bolted on the inside. Shevill woke up in his bed to find Curry on top of him 'possing' him, that is to say beating him with hands and knees. Curry then cut Shevill's throat with a razor, causing a wound described later in the murder indictment as four inches long and three inches deep. The razor belonged to Robert Shevill and had been taken from a cupboard downstairs at the inn. Curry then ran away from the premises and Robert Shevill staggered downstairs and managed to reach 'Mrs Hopley's house' nearby.

There was clear suspicion from the outset that someone must have let Curry into the Three Horseshoes and it may be significant that Shevill did not go to his wife for help after being wounded by Curry. Mary Hall, a servant living in at the establishment, said she had checked the doors of the inn were locked on the Wednesday night before going to Isabel Shevill's bedroom. Hall said she slept on a 'truckle bedd' (a low bed fitted with wheels that could be moved and stored under a higher bed.) next to the bed of her mistress. She was disturbed by the noise in the early hours of Thursday morning. Mrs Shevill was then asleep and the bedroom door was fastened from the inside. Hall went out of the inn and saw Robert Shevill at the house of Mrs Hopley. Shevill had dreadful injuries to his throat and could hardly speak but managed to make her understand the words 'Molly,

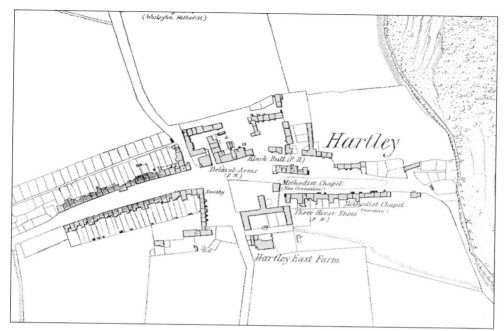

Hartley Village and the Three Horseshoes.

clear yourself.' Hall went back to rouse Mrs Shevill who said to her 'Molly, I am afraid of waking the child, but in case your master has been murdered, he has murdered himself.' If all of what Hall said were true and she neither heard nor saw anything else of importance why was Robert Shevill, with his dreadful injuries, moved to say to her 'Molly clear yourself'? But she revealed nothing else except that strange remark attributed to Isabel Shevill suggesting suicide.

The day after the attack Robert Shevill, on his death bed, gave a written statement in the presence of seven witnesses describing how Curry had attacked him. No one was found who saw Michael Curry in the Three Horseshoes or in any part of Hartley at the time of the assault. Thomas Oliver and John Gibson, two men lodging at Mrs Hopley's house in Hartley, confirmed that Robert Shevill came to the house about three o'clock in the morning crying out 'Murder.' They saw that his throat was cut in several places. Shevill gestured for a pen, ink and paper to be brought to him and he wrote down particulars of who had injured him. Thomas Oliver went at once to see Isabel Shevill at the Three Horseshoes. She asked Oliver what was the matter and he challenged by saying, 'You must certainly know whatever was the matter', but Mrs Shevill said nothing.

Isabel Shevill showed an extraordinary lack of interest and concern for the welfare of her husband; no one spoke of her rendering the assistance and aid that one might expect from a loving and supportive wife. The disturbance and noise at Mrs Hopley's house attracted the attention of John Murray of Hartley, who was on his way to work at that early hour. Murray saw the injuries to Shevill, heard him accuse Curry of responsibility and saw Shevill 'write a paper purporting to be a discovery of the person who had wounded him which paper this Informant believes is now in the Custody of Mr Nich's Armstrong.'

Robert Shevill had an illegitimate son called Nicholas Armstrong living in the village. John Gibson, after speaking to Mrs Shevill, went at once to tell Armstrong what had happened and bring him to help his father. It was Armstrong who took possession of the notes written by his father accusing Michael Curry. Later that morning, Shevill was moved back to the Three Horseshoes and put to bed. He was visited about nine o'clock by a close friend, John Wheatley. It was an emotional meeting between these friends. Amongst other things, Shevill said to him 'Jonny you are too late a coming for Michael Currey has murdered me and several times after that he said Oh I shall dye, and Michael Currey is the cause of my Death he has killed Me.'

Then followed an interesting example of how 18th century crime investigation was carried out. It fell to the parish constable Dennis Graydon, an unpaid, untrained parish appointment, to take steps to find the suspect and bring him before a magistrate. Other members of the community were required to help as needed. About the same time on the Thursday morning that John Wheatley was visiting Robert Shevill, Graydon together with Nicholas Armstrong and Matthew Brown went to Ralph Curry's house at Low Lights at North Shields seeking his son Michael Curry. They found the wanted man in bed and arrested him. They also found blood-stained stockings belonging to Michael Curry drying before the fire in the house. His shoes were wet and dirty.

They took Curry back to the Three Horseshoes and brought him before Robert Shevill, who declared in his presence that Michael Curry had cut his throat. Curry then said 'Who me?' Shevill answered, 'Yes, you did it.'

The local justices of the peace, Matthew White and Nicholas Fenwick,

North Shields around 1829.

promptly set about their business and on the Thursday took depositions from Mary Hall, Thomas Oliver, John Gibson, John Murray and Ralph Curry in open court session. They also examined the prisoner, Michael Curry, in accordance with the practice of the day. The prisoner denied wounding Robert Shevill and gave a detailed account of his movements for the whole week. He claimed he had spent the evening of the attack on the quay at South Shields. He stayed there for about two hours with some sailors from Whitby and six or seven others who were smugglers. At about midnight or 1am, he returned to his father's house and went to bed where he stayed until he was arrested at about 9am the next day.

On Friday 12 January 1738/39 the justices took further depositions from John Wheatley, Nicholas Armstrong and Matthew Brown. No evidence from Isabel Shevill has survived but it is clear from a newspaper report the next day that the justices had decided to charge Michael Curry and Isabel Shevill with wounding Robert Shevill. They were committed into the care of the county gaoler, William Lowes, at the Northumberland County Gaol in Bridge Street, Morpeth.

> They write from Morpeth that on Thursday night last one Michael
> Curry, a lodger at one Robert Shevell's at Hartley in the County of
> Northumberland, cut the throat and other parts of the body of the said
> Shevell, with a razor, for which he was committed to Morpeth Gaol by
> the Bench of justices then holding the Sessions; and tis said that the
> said Shevell's wife, is also charged with, and committed for the same.
>
> *Newcastle Courant* Saturday 13 January 1738/39

Robert Shevill died at Hartley on Saturday 13 January, 1738/39 and was
buried the following Monday. Death in such tragic circumstances required
the usual formal enquiry by the Coroner and his jury returned a verdict of
murder by Michael Curry; which in turn led to the Coroner issuing an
indictment against Curry for murder.

> Last Saturday dy'd Robert Shevell, whose throat was mention'd to be
> cut in our last by one Michael Curry: Since which the Coroners Jury
> have brought in their verdict, Wilful Murder; and the said Curry, with
> the deceased's wife (on suspicion of being an accomplice) are in
> Morpeth Gaol for the same.
>
> *Newcastle Courant* Saturday 20 January 1738/39

The next Assizes for Northumberland began in the Moot Hall in
Castlegarth on Monday 20 August 1739 before Thomas Parker. The formal
indictment for murder against Michael Curry and Isabel Shevill was a
typical 18th century document of its kind, asserting that these two people
acted 'not having the fear of God before their eyes and seduced by the
instigation of the Devil.' The indictment charged Curry with actually
committing the murder of Robert Shevill by cutting his throat, and charged
Isabel Shevill with aiding and abetting Curry. The original document in the
Public Record office is endorsed 'True Bill as to Michael Curry, No Bill as to
Isabel Shevil.' This endorsement indicates that the Northumberland Grand

Jury found there was a substantive case against Curry to go forward for a full trial before the Judge sitting with a petit jury (twelve men) to come to a verdict. But 'No Bill' for Isabel Shevill meant the matter went no further, she was entitled to be released forthwith.

No account of the trial of Curry has survived but there is a further endorsement against Curry's name on the original indictment 'puts guilty.' This indicates that after the trial of Michael Curry the jury found him guilty of murder as charged. The judge, Baron Parker, pronounced the death sentence against Curry and that was formally recorded in the official court records as quoted at the opening of this chapter.

There were actually four death sentences passed at the Northumberland and Newcastle upon Tyne Assizes in August of 1739, all for murder:

> **Newcastle Aug. 24th On Monday last began, and this Day ended the Assizes, for this Town, and the County of Northumberland: two persons received sentence of death at the Town-court, and two at the Moot Hall, viz, Thomas Pearson and William Smith, both of this place, the former for the Murder of Robert Langstaff and the latter for the Murder of his Wife. At the Moot Hall John Wilson for the Murder of Barbara Trumble, and Michael Curry, for the Murder of Robert Sheavel. Six were ordered for Transportation.**
>
> *Newcastle Courant* Saturday 25 August 1739

Thomas Pearson was reprieved and later transported for 14 years, William Smith, as a Newcastle upon Tyne offender, was hanged on the Town Moor, Newcastle on Friday 14 September 1739.

The Northumberland County officials made arrangements for Michael Curry and John Wilson to be hanged outside the West Gate at Newcastle upon Tyne in a double execution. The date fixed was Tuesday 4 September 1739. When required the Northumberland gallows was set up at Newcastle on county land.

The *Newcastle Courant* carried a short report, but the *Newcastle Journal* gave a much more detailed and interesting account of the executions, but there is some uncertainty about which day in the week the executions were carried out:

Last Wednesday [i.e. 5 September 1739] were executed at the West Gate near this place (who received Sentence of Death at the last Assizes for the County of Northumberland) Michael Curry and John Wilson, the former for the murder of Robert Shevell of Hartley, and the latter for the Murder of Barbara Trumble of Donclaywood; they both owned the Facts for which they suffered and behaved well under their unhappy Circumstances. The Body of Curry was afterwards hung in chains near Hartley; Wilson was buried in the Back-part of St. John's Churchyard

Newcastle Courant Saturday 8 September 1739

On Tuesday last [i.e. Tuesday 4 September 1739] were executed without Westgate near this town Michael Curry and John Wilson; they behaved decently tho' they met their unhappy fate without any apparent terror of Death. Neither of them made any Speech or Confession at the Place of Execution; but some time before delivered what they thought proper to say in writing to the Rev. Mr Wilkinson. From a Copy of which, printed by Mr White, it appears that Curry owned himself Guilty of the Murder charged upon him; but his expressions clear the Wife (now the Widow) of Sheavel from inveigling or enticing him to any very sinful Acts, and of persuading him to injure her husband. In Extenuation of his own Guilt, he has declared (and appeal'd to the World for the Truth of it) that he was always, before committing the aforesaid Murder, a regular, laborious, honest Man, and had the grace to keep the Sabbath Day holy tho' he owns himself guilty of breaking several other commandments by Swearing, Drinking &c. As to the Murder of Sheevel, he has not fully explained the Motives that induced him to it; but he has asserted he did not commit in so Bloody and Barbarous a manner as represented; for he did not bring a Razor with him, but found it; which Razor he says made the Wounds, but he did not put his fingers in them. He once desisted from his cruel purpose, which upon further Deliberation he executed. But he begs Leave to declare the Evidences at his trial swore to some things which were not true … Curry's body was carried directly from the place of Execution to Hartley and hung in chains.

Newcastle Journal Saturday 8 September 1739

The generally accepted date is Tuesday 4 September 1739 and both accounts indicate that Curry did accept his guilt of the murder, exonerated Isabel Shevill but at the end of it all he did not fully explain his reasons for the attack on Robert Shevill. After the execution was complete Curry's body was taken down and carried to the coast, encased in a bag of chains and put up on a gibbet. Usually a gibbet would be erected within sight of the scene of the crime and the body would be left in place until it rotted away. The place chosen for Curry's gibbet was the edge of the coast where the causeway begins leading across to St Mary's Island. It was a dramatic and exposed location and the gibbet could be clearly seen from the Three Horseshoes just across the bay at Hartley.

Whether Isabel Shevill returned to the Three Horseshoes is not known but it continued as an inn for many years and was last mentioned in the district directories in the 19th century.

In 1769, 30 years after the execution, Andrew Armstrong published his fine series of maps of the county of Northumberland. By that time the headland at St. Mary's Island was already known as Curry's Point. It was marked as Curry's Point on Armstrong's map for that part of the coast and that name has continued to be used through to the 21st century.

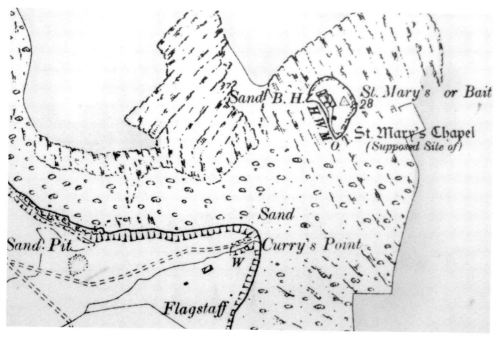

It is one of life's ironies that Curry should have one of the most picturesque landmarks on the Northumbrian coastline named after him, whilst his victim was buried in obscurity in the parish churchyard. The 250th anniversary of the gibbet was marked in 1989 by the erection of stone plinth with a blue commemoration plaque bearing the following inscription:

On 4th September 1739
Michael Curry was executed for the murder of the landlord
of the Three Horseshoes Inn Hartley.
His body was afterwards hung in chains from a gibbet
at this spot within sight of the scene of the crime.
Ever since that gruesome event this headland has been known as
Curry's Point.
Erected 4th September 1989 to mark the 250th Anniversary

3. Sentence of the Court

CHRISTMAS SESSIONS 12th JANUARY 1791

William Rutter and John Charlton. Ordered that the Treasurer pay them Three pounds, four shillings and two pence for three coffins for James Greenwood, John Brown and George Bolton convicted of felony at last Assizes and for work done at the Gaol for this county.

(Northumberland Quarter Sessions Order Book 1786-1793 QSO 13)

This sombre entry in the county records points to the key element of the punishment strategy in the United Kingdom in the 18th century. It was the time of what was known as the 'Bloody Code', a string of statutes that brought the death penalty to well over 200 offences. Almost every edition of the Tyneside newspapers carried reports of executions somewhere in the country. Northumberland had its share, although the numbers were not large, 28 men and three women in the century; the first was Michael Curry in 1739 for murder, and the last Walter Clarke and Margaret Dunn in 1793 for separate burglaries. Four men and two women were hanged for murder, and the rest for a wide range of offences including highway robbery, arson, coining, breaking and entering various premises, stealing sheep and horses and one for returning unlawfully from transportation. Many of the stories are told in detail elsewhere in this book. Around 75 per cent of those sentenced to death at the Northumberland Assizes were actually reprieved later and ordered for transportation, usually for life or 14 years.

All of these serious crime trials took place in the old Moot Hall Court at Castlegarth, Newcastle upon Tyne before a high court judge. The Moot Hall was a very old building, pulled down in 1810, and little is known about the inside of it. According to M. Ross (*Architectural and Picturesque Views of*

Castlegarth and Moot Hall, 1746.
Right, the 13th century Moot Hall.

Newcastle upon Tyne 1841): 'The
benches, docks, &c., for the trial of
criminal and civil cases, were fitted
up at the south and north ends
respectively; and it was not
uncommon for two trials to be
going on at the same time.'

The county had two sites for a
gallows in the 18th century. The
first was at the modern junction of
Westgate Road and Bath Lane, Newcastle, which, at that time, was shire
county land outside the walls of the town. This was a short distance for the

The West Gate and the site of the gallows in 1786.

execution procession to travel from the dungeon at the Keep. It was sometimes necessary to carry out executions within two or three days of sentence, for murder for example. There was no appeal system at that time. There was one attempt during the 18th century to move the county gallows from outside the West Gate.

MIDSUMMER QUARTER SESSIONS 16th JULY 1760

The Gallows for this County. Ordered that the same be removed from the Place where it now stands near the Westgate to some more convenient place between the said Westgate and the Quarry House.

(Northumberland CRO, Quarter Sessions Order Book 1754 – 1765 QSO 9)

This order was not actually carried out and further executions took place up to 1811 when the West Gate was demolished and other changes took place.

There are records in the Newcastle upon Tyne Parish Registers of executions taking place on county land at Castlegarth during the 17th century, but none later than that. The second location for county executions was at Morpeth. At Easter 1727 the justices at the Quarter Sessions ordered the county surveyor to erect a gallows at Morpeth.

NORTHUMBERLAND QUARTER SESSIONS ORDER BOOK 1727-1742

Easter Sessions 1727

Gallows for the execution of Malefactors. Ordered That one be made & erected at Morpeth near the county Gaole by the Surveyor at the county's charge.

(Northumberland Record Office Access No. QSO 7)

This order may have said 'near the county Gaole' but in fact the county gallows was on the outskirts of Morpeth at a place called Fair Moor on the road leading north out of the town. The opening quotation of this chapter links to a triple execution in 1790.

Wednesday 18th August 1790.

John Brown, for breaking into a house at Fenham; James Greenwood, for breaking into a shop at North Sunderland; and George Bolton, for horse-stealing, were executed at Morpeth. The execution of three criminals at one time drew an immense multitude of spectators. Brown was born at Winlaton, in the county of Durham, and left a widow and six children. Greenwood left a widow and three children. Bolton was born at Usworth in the county of Durham, and had lived as a servant with several people at North Shields.

(*Local Records or Historical Register* John Sykes, 1835, Page 356)

William Rutter and John Charlton were paid to erect a gallows at Morpeth in 1788 to hang John and Robert Winter, father and son. It seems likely to have been the same gallows at Fair Moor used for the three men hanged in 1790. There is little information in the archives to identify a hangman for county executions, except in 1792, when a fellow convict was used to hang William Winter and the Clarke sisters at West Gate. The first executions at Morpeth in the 18th century were as late as 1742, when John Todd and William Simpson were hanged there for sheep stealing. Of the executions quoted earlier, 18 men and one woman were hanged at Morpeth between 1742 and 1790.

The judges could exercise two further options linked to executions for murder. The first was to order the display of the executed murder's body on a gibbet. There were just two examples from the Northumberland Assizes of the 18th century, Michael Curry in 1739 and William Winter in 1792. Gibbets were a common sight around the country at that time, with the body covered in pitch and held together in a bag of chains or iron bands to preserve this gruesome warning for as long as possible, sometimes with unexpected results.

Extraordinary circumstance – About seven years ago a man was gibbeted on Saxelby Moor for the murder of his wife. In his mouth has recently been found a bird's nest with young and what is more remarkable, the same species of bird (a willow biter) built her nest there last season.

[Saxelby is in Leicestershire]

Newcastle Advertizer Thursday 13 August 1812

The last person to be gibbeted in the north east of England was William Jobling. He was hanged at Durham on 1 August 1832 for the murder of Nicholas Fairles Esq. The body of Jobling was afterwards gibbeted at Jarrow on a gibbet placed in the River Tyne below the high water mark so that the body was submerged at high tide. However the body soon disappeared from the gibbet, probably removed by friends for burial. That was just ten days before the last condemned criminal was gibbeted in this country. He was James Cook, hanged at Leicester on 11 August 1832 for murder and gibbeted at Aylestone, Leicester. The practice of gibbeting offenders was formally ended on 25 July 1834.

The other option for the judges was to order that the body of the executed felon be passed to the local surgeons to be 'dissected and anatomised'. Of the six Northumberland murderers hanged in the 18th century, the bodies of one man and two women were given to the surgeons, two men were gibbeted and the sixth was simply buried in St John's churchyard at Newcastle upon Tyne. There was no problem about burying executed criminals in hallowed ground, although tradition has it that they were interred on the north side in the shadow of the church so that the grave would never be fully warmed by the sun. Dissection orders of this kind for Northumberland and Newcastle upon Tyne Assizes led to the bodies being passed to the Barber Surgeons' Hall near the Holy Jesus Hospital at Newcastle. The body was dissected in public with lectures by the surgeons on the various organs.

The Barber Surgeons' Hall, Newcastle.

In 1753 three men were convicted at the Northumberland Assizes of the rape of a woman who died of her injuries a few months later. They were ordered for execution followed by dissection of their bodies. Generally speaking there was no appeal system at that time, but the judges were persuaded to stay the execution and eventually the men were pardoned. The county record of the pardon has survived and the wording of the document reveals just how pressure and representations on behalf of the condemned men could alter the course of justice.

NORTHUMBERLAND QUARTER SESSIONS ORDER BOOK 1742-1753
George R.

Whereas Job Lawson, William Hall and John Walker were at the last Assizes held for our County of Northumberland tried for and found guilty of the Murder of Elizabeth Hall and received Sentence of Death for the same. But upon Contrariety of Evidence appearing in their favour at their Trial and many of Grand Jury and other Gentlemen of Distinction earnestly requesting a Respite of their sentence, they were afterwards reprieved for Two Months by the Judge before whom they were tried, and whereas We have since thought fit upon Consideration of the Premises and Some other Circumstances humbly represented unto us on their Behalf, further Respite the Execution of their Said Sentence. And are now graciously pleased to extend them our Free Pardon for the Said Crime. Our will and Pleasure therefore is, That you cause them the said Job Lawson, William Hall, John Walker, to be inserted for the said crime in our first and next General Pardon that shall come out for the Northern Circuit without any Condition whatsoever; And that in the Meantime you take Bail for their Appearances, in Order to Plead our said Pardon, and for so doing This shall be our Warrant, Given at Our Court of St. James the Third Day of January in the 27th Year of our Reign

By His Majesty's Command

Holles Newcastle

To our Trusty and Well Beloved our Justices of Assize for the Northern Circuit,

Our Sheriff of Our County of Northumberland

and all Others whom it may concern.

(Northumberland Record Office Access No. QSO 8, final page)

A common way of escaping punishment, including the death penalty, in the 18th century was pleading benefit of clergy (privilegium clericale, Blackstones Commentaries). This was an ancient right to claim membership of the clergy by proof of literacy, that is to say by reading or reciting the opening verse of Psalm 51. Members of the clergy could only be punished by an ecclesiastic court, which did not have the death penalty, and not by the judges of the lay courts. The claim to benefit of clergy was made after conviction but before sentence. After being granted benefit of clergy the prisoners were then 'burnt in the hand', that is to say branded, usually at the base of the left thumb with a letter 'F' for felon, to prevent a second claim and then released. There are many examples in the Northumberland and Newcastle upon Tyne Assize records. A Northumberland blacksmith escaped punishment in 1748 for a particularly macabre murder.

(At the Northumberland Assizes at the Moot Hall in Castlegarth.)

William SPARK, blacksmith, for murder of Samuel DOVE by running a red-hot iron rod into his body was found guilty of manslaughter and was burnt in the hand.

Newcastle Courant Saturday 13 August 1748

The branding of such prisoners was the end of the matter.

The high court judges had the widest possible powers of punishment but the pattern of sentences at the county and town courts were consistent year after year, death or transportation was the order of the day. Occasionally the judges may order prisoners to be whipped or pilloried before transportation, but that was not common. Assize prisoners were facing one of two options, death or transportation to the colonies in North America or the West Indies in the early part of the 18th century, then later to Australia. The rapid growth of transportation in the early days explains the strange lack of executions in the early part of the century. It is apparent from the statistics that the judges were encouraged to stay the execution of condemned criminals thought suitable for transportation. Then the practice was formally included in the Transportation Act of 1717/18 (4 Geo I cII). There are records showing that in the first 35 years of the 18th century at least 69 convicts were sentenced to transportation by the Northumberland and Newcastle upon Tyne Courts and 28 of those convicts had been reprieved from the death sentence (*Emigrants in Bondage*, Peter Wilson Coldham, 1988).

The Transportation Act also reduced the effects of 'Benefit of Clergy' for several offences including grand and petit larceny, by enabling the courts to transport such convicts in addition to being 'burnt in the hand'. The effect of this new act was seen at once at the Northumberland Assizes on 3 August 1718/19 when a man called John alias George Scott was convicted of felony. Details of his exact offence have not survived. Scott was liable to have been branded on the hand as the only punishment for his offence but now, under the new act, was transported to the American Colonies.

From the third decade of the 18th century executions begin to appear again at regular intervals, although the judges still reprieved many prisoners from the death sentence for transportation. As may be seen from the following statistics, more prisoners were sentenced directly to that punishment. Analysing the sentences (195) in a random 10 per cent sample of the Northumberland and Newcastle upon Tyne Assizes in the 18th century reveals the major groups as: Death 4.6 per cent; Death but reprieved for transportation 12.8 per cent; Transported 14.4 per cent; Burnt in the hand (Benefit of Clergy) 6.1 per cent; Discharged or Acquitted 35 per cent; No Bill found 4.1 per cent and Remanded 9.8 per cent. Identifying 45.2 per cent of the sample as discharged, acquitted, no bill found, or escaping punishment through benefit of clergy, is a disturbing statistic and raises a huge question mark over the efficiency of the 18th century enforcement and trial system.

The arrangements for transporting the convicts were made by two local justices, formally nominated at the Quarter Sessions, entering into a contract between the county and government-approved national agents who for a fee, typically £5 per head, collected the prisoners by ship from the Tyne. In the case of John alias George Scott mentioned above, for example, the Northumberland Justices were 'ffrancis Rudston and John Reed', contracting with 'John Darley of Gray's Inn in the County of Middlesex Esq. and John Hendon of Lincoln's Inn in the County of Middlesex aforesaid'. The prisoners were taken south to join other convicts from around the country. The ships were adapted for the purpose and, given favourable conditions, took about three weeks to cross the Atlantic. The convicts were then sold on to plantation owners seeking labourers. It follows labour supplied in this way was not of good quality. As the colonies developed the authorities protested long and hard about being a dumping ground for the gaols of the United Kingdom. Returning unlawfully from transportation was a capital crime. Occasionally the county gaoler would have to move prisoners by land to ports further away from Morpeth than the Tyne. There are records of John Blake, the county gaoler, making journeys with transportees as far as Gravesend and Portsmouth. No explanation survives as to why such awkward journeys were necessary.

The justices of Northumberland sitting as the 'Quarter Sessions of the Peace' exercised a wider variety of punishments than the high court judges. No power to use the death penalty for them, of course, but the justices frequently sentenced prisoners to be transported. The sessions of January 1751/52 in the Town Hall at Morpeth, includes an example of a troublesome prisoner dealt with in a different way.

Northumberland Quarter Sessions Order Books 1742 – 1753

Christmas Sessions 15th January 1751/2 held at Morpeth.

Robert Armstrong of Mount Hexley being convicted at this sessions of petty Larceny. It is ordered that he be transported to some of his Majesties Colonies and Plantations in America for the term of seven years.

Elizabeth Rochester being convicted at this sessions of petty Larceny. It is ordered that she be whipt through the town of Morpeth next Market Day then sent to her legall settlement by a vagrants pass.

(Northumberland Record Office Access No. QSO 8)

Elizabeth Rochester learned little from this experience. In August 1754 she was convicted at Durham Assizes of housebreaking and stealing money and the judge sentenced her to be transported for seven years. She escaped from Durham Gaol but was recaptured and the following year duly transported to America. Rochester was fortunate not to lose her life, as escaping from gaol after sentence of transportation was a capital offence. She was described as 'one of the gang of Faws, or strolling predators, who infested the northern counties at this period'. A final example shows that neither whipping nor the pillory was sufficient to deter some women from re-offending.

July 20th 1771.

Christian Horsley, who had been convicted at Quarter sessions, in Newcastle,

of obtaining goods on false pretences, stood this day from twelve o'clock to one o'clock, exalted on a pillory on the Sandhill. At the quarter sessions held in Alnwick*, in the following October, this woman received sentence of transportation for defrauding Miss Pye, a milliner, at Morpeth, of goods of the value of £3. [* at the Town Hall, Alnwick]

(*Local Records or Historical Register,* John Sykes, 1835, Page 281)

There were pillories and stocks in all the towns of the North East. At North Shields for example:

At the Quarter Sessions held at Morpeth on Monday last George Embleton was convicted of obtaining money under false pretences from three butchers in Shields and sentenced to stand in the pillory for one hour at North Shields on Saturday 16th instant.

Newcastle Chronicle Saturday 9 April 1785

The pillory was far more dangerous than the stocks. The offender was secured by the head and hands and could not protect himself if pelted with stones or rocks. If the man became unconscious, death by strangulation could follow. In the stocks, on the other hand, the offender's feet were held fast but he could protect himself to a degree with his hands. The object of this use of the stocks and pillory was not to set up the offender as some sort of 'Aunt Sally' for the amusement of the community, but to exhibit the offenders in humiliation and try to bring about a change in their behaviour. The stocks were used to deal with public nuisances of the local or parish variety such as drunkenness, traders selling short measure and the like. There are many historical references

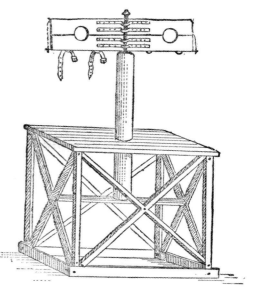

in Northumberland, including a strange use of the stocks at Corbridge in 1293.

Northumberland Assizes 1293

CORBRIDGE. Adam, son of Questrygg of Matfen put in the stocks for an hour, for wounding a man who died three months later, then bailed to the Assize, said to be dead at the time of the Assize.

(*History of Northumberland*, Northumberland History Committee 1914.)

Villages were required to maintain a stocks under the supervision of the parish constable. The growing community of Westgate outside the town walls of Newcastle was ordered to set up a stocks in 1693 or face a penalty.

Northumberland Quarter Sessions Order Books 1677 – 1697

Adjourned Quarter Sessions 18th February 1691, Westgate

A new pair of stocks to be erected at Westgate by the inhabitants by the next sessions or forfeit 40 shillings.

(Northumberland Record Office Access No. QSO 2)

Preserved in the Mayor's Parlour at Morpeth today there is a strange device called the branks, a sort of open helmet of metal straps that was put on the heads of women who spread false and malicious gossip. It was fixed over the head with a piece of metal fitted into the woman's mouth to keep her tongue still. The last recorded use was at Morpeth in 1741 on Elizabeth Holborn for 'scandalous and opprobrious language.' She was led around the Market Place for two hours. Fines for petty offences were common at the Northumberland Sessions, usually one shilling or two shillings and sixpence – the old half crown. Occasionally the justices displayed ingenuity in their sentences. At Morpeth Town Hall in January 1741/42 John Hutchinson of 'Blackeburn' appeared at the sessions on two charges of petty theft and pleaded

guilty. The record of the sentence reads 'enlisted in court as a soldier' (NCRO QS07). The words 'in court' show a canny Northumbrian approach by the justices, ensuring this offender had been sworn into the military before leaving the court. On another occasion, in 1749, James Watson for stealing a blanket and other things was recorded as 'in gaole and sent away by pass.' In other words the justices were using the parish pass system, for sending vagrants to their legal domicile, to get rid of Watson out of their jurisdiction. One wonders what the reaction was of the authorities at Watson's destination, wherever that may have been.

One example of whipping has already been given and this practice of inflicting pain and public humiliation was frequently used to deal with a wide range of offenders throughout Northumberland in the 18th century. The offender was stripped to the waist, tied by the hands to the back of a cart and whipped around the town, often on a route prescribed by the justices. The whipping posts favoured elsewhere were not used in the north east. It was also common to link a whipping to a spell in the house of correction.

Christmas Session, 13th January 1741, Morpeth

Margory ffoster of North Shields, Spinster, for stealing a web* of striped Linen, the goods of Nicholas Charlton, value 10d.

Guilty. To be publickly whipt and com'td to the house of correction for 3 mths.

(NCRO QS07

[*a woven piece of cloth.]

At the General Quarter Sessions of the Peace, held at Alnwick in and for the county of Northumberland, on Wednesday 3 October 1787

At the above sessions
Mary Gladstones, of Alnwick, single-woman, found guilty of petit larceny, was committed to the house of correction at Morpeth, to hard labour, for one month, and then whipped through the town of Alnwick, and discharged:

Mary Clarke, of Alnwick, single-woman, found guilty of petit larceny, was committed to the house of correction at Morpeth and there to be privately whipped, and then discharged:

Newcastle Courant Saturday 6 October 1787

Here was typical 18th century strategy at work, the notion of bringing about reform by inflicting severe pain and humiliation in a very public way, followed by confinement and hard labour. Imprisonment in the county gaol as a sentence was rarely used. The house of correction, a mixture of confinement, discipline, spartan conditions, tight supervision and hard work was seen as the right road to reform for the 18th century.

Finally, here is another example of combining whipping with hard labour, this time with the aim of stamping out the pilfering of coal from a riverside staith at North Shields.

Wednesday [10 January 1787] at the General Quarter Sessions of the Peace, was held at Morpeth, for the County of Northumberland when William Hodgson of South Shields, Scullerman, was convicted for feloniously taking a quantity of coals from off Whitehill Point Staith, the property of Messrs Errington and Ward, between the hours of one and two o'clock on the morning of the 19th of last month; and sentenced to be committed to the house of correction at Morpeth, for three months, to hard labour, and till the Wednesday following; when he is to be whipped thro' the town of North Shields, and then discharged. It is to be hoped that this will put a stop to such daring offenders, who have long made a practice of pilfering the Staiths below the Bridge; the Owners of which, we are given to understand, intend immediately to enter into an association to prosecute to the utmost vigour of the law, all such persons, who shall be guilty of taking any of their property from Staiths, Wagonways, Collieries &c.

Newcastle Courant Saturday 13 January 1787

4. Winter's Gibbet

> The nefarious activities of the gang of Winter are too well known,
> and unhappily the effects have been too much felt, particularly in the
> western parts of Northumberland and struck so much terror
> into the minds of the inhabitants as to excite the highest detestation
> and abhorrance of that vile community and called forth on this
> occasion universal indignation.
>
> (Winter Gang Broadsheet August 1792)

A mile or so south of Elsdon in mid-Northumberland, high on the moors on the old turnpike road leading to Hartburn, Wallington and Morpeth stands the grim Northumbrian landmark 'Winter's Gibbet' (right). It takes its name from William Winter, the leader of the gang who, late in the 18th century, carried out a dreadful burglary and murder in that part of the county.

Five miles north of the gibbet and to the left of the road leading from Elsdon to Rothbury stands an ancient pele tower, now built into a cluster of farm buildings

Barry Redfern

The pele tower at the Raw.

called The Raw. The building is, strictly speaking, a bastle but invariably was referred to as a pele in the reports on the Winter case. In the desperate times of border troubles livestock would be herded into the ground floor of the building and secured for safety whilst the people took refuge in the upper room.

In August of 1791 Margaret Crozier, a widow, lived in the pele, she was said to be 'infirm through age' (the conventional spelling of Crozier is used here, but there was much variation in the reports and records of the time). Margaret Crozier supported herself by keeping a shop for her countryside neighbours and travellers, and stocked a wide variety of goods, clothing, tobacco, and foodstuff including such things as currants, raisins and green peas.

A neighbour, Barbara Drummond, spent some time with Margaret Crozier on the evening of Monday 29 August 1791 and 'left her in good health and spirits about nine o'clock'. Barbara Drummond returned there the following morning, between seven and eight o'clock; the outer door was standing open and she called out for Mrs Crozier but receiving no answer went away. An hour later she went back to the pele and entered, calling for the shopkeeper. There was no answer and Barbara Drummond saw cupboards and chests standing open and clothing lying about the floor.

She called neighbours for help; they went back and found Margaret Crozier lying dead inside her bed. It was an old style cupboard bed with doors on it. The dead woman's face was bloody. Another neighbour, Eleanor Young, came into the house and they found that a red and white spotted handkerchief was tied tightly around Margaret Crozier's neck and knotted three times. Young unfastened the handkerchief and, as she disturbed the bedclothes, a knife fell onto the floor.

It was described as a cooper's gulley knife, with a six-inch blade and a long wooden haft or handle closed by an iron hoop next to the blade. There was blood on the knife and trapped between the handle and the blade of the knife was a piece of straw 'about the length of a thumb nail.'

The shop storage cupboards had been turned out onto the floor and Mrs Crozier's neighbours could see at glance that food and clothing were missing. The alarm was raised; messages went to Rothbury for the surgeons, and to the Coroner and the parish elders. The parish constable was called.

William Wilson and Samuel Davison, surgeons of Rothbury, arrived to examine Margaret Crozier. They found a wound under her right eye, livid spots on her cheeks and jaw, a slight scratch on the right side of her neck, and 'a fracture and depression on the right temple about two thirds of an inch long; that the jugular veins were turgid and a swelling under the left ear; that her neck had the appearance as if she had been strangled', and the surgeons expressed the opinion that 'the fracture with depression aforesaid was the cause of the death of Margaret Crozier.' Margaret Crozier had been savagely beaten and strangled.

The parish constable for Elsdon at that time was John Brown, aged 36, the son of a farmer at Laing Hill near the Raw. He was a second cousin of Lancelot 'Capability' Brown of Ravenscleugh, the landscape gardener. The Coroner for the county, Collingwood Forster Lindsay, an attorney, instructed John Brown to summon an inquest jury for the following day Wednesday 31 August 1791. The body of Margaret Crozier was then moved out of the Pele and into a room in John Jackson's house at the Raw and 'Which Jury was summoned and did sit upon the Said body of the Said Margaret Crozier the same day.' (That is to say in the presence of the body.)

At the inquest it was the evidence of two shepherd boys, Robert Hindmarsh (or Hymers), aged 11-and-a-half years, and Abraham Best, an infant, that was to spark off a manhunt around the county of Northumberland. Hindmarsh told the coroner that on the Monday afternoon before the murder they were looking after sheep on Whisker Shield Common (now known as 'Whiskershiel') near Elsdon. They saw a tall man and two stout young women eating food in a sheepfold on top of a hill.

The man and the two women had an ass with them and the boys observed the man putting a 'happing' (a kind of covering) and a sack onto it. The man saw the boys and asked the time, which they estimated was between 3.30 and 4pm. The boys saw a knife with a long blade and long wooden handle lying on the ground beside these people. One of the women picked up the knife, wound some straw around it and put it into the sack on the ass. The man and the women then set off walking to the north on a route that would bring them to the Raw in around an hour. It is significant to note that the boys said that the man was standing upright all the time they observed him. They identified the knife found in Margaret Crozier's bed as the one they had seen on Whisker Shield Common.

George Hedley, a farmer of East Nook near Elsdon, told the Coroner that he had found footmarks of a man or men, and a woman or women and of an ass at a stone wall about one mile south of the Raw on the Tuesday morning. The same morning Hedley had also found currants, raisins, starch and green peas lying near a pike of hay at East Nook, about four miles south of the Raw. Next to them was a fresh mark of a woman's heel of a particular shape he had never seen before.

The inquest jury returned a verdict of murder and the coroner handed the knife into the care of John Brown and directed him 'to find out, if he could, to whom it belonged and by what means it came thereat.' The Coroner also gave instructions that 'a meeting should be held at Elsdon for the purpose of considering and taking the best steps of discovering of the aforesaid Murder.'

That meeting and the funeral of Margaret Crozier took place the following day Thursday 1 September 1791 at St Cuthbert's Parish Church, Elsdon. The Rector of Elsdon was absent from the parish so the responsibility fell on Richard Harrison, the curate, who chaired the vestry meeting recorded in the parish accounts book as follows:

At a vestry meeting now held in consequence of a shocking and inhuman murder committed upon the body of Margaret Crozier of the Raw, in this parish, by certain persons known to be vagrants and suspected persons are believed to have been the perpetrators of the above Act: We the Ministers, Overseers, Churchwardens and principal inhabitants do agree to appoint proper persons to go immediately to different districts within ye County in order to search for and apprehend the said suspicious persons (who were two women and one man travelling with a Dunn Ass) and also provide that persons in the search shall be reimbursed their necessary expenses by ye Parish at large and that they do herewith proceed with all expedition to do the above business.

(Northumberland Record Office Access No. EP83/18)

Groups of men led by parish constables set out in four different directions to search for the suspects. A group of three men led by John Brown set off south about ten o'clock on the Thursday morning, 2 September, going to Redchester, Kirk Whelpington and Kirk Harle. They rode many miles, searching and enquiring. Brown soon found that he was on the right track. Residents, shopkeepers and alehouse proprietors told him they had seen one man and two women, fitting the description of the suspects, heading north on Monday 29 August, with an ass, then the same group making their way south the following morning with the ass now heavily laden. Brown also learned that the tall dark man had bought himself a fresh pair of shoes at Kirk Whelpington from a shopkeeper called Thomas Mitchilson.

John Brown's party rested overnight at Nafferton and the next day went to Horsley Moor, where he saw a woman vagrant with two asses going on towards Horsley. Some distance behind this woman there was a man looking after a pony. Brown realised that the man and woman fitted the descriptions given by the shepherd boys. He secured assistance from other people working on the moor and took the man into custody first. The man declared himself to be William Cameron, a pitman from Wylam. In fact 'Cameron' was a man named William Winter, who was said to have spent less than six months free from prison in the previous 18 years. In August 1784 William Winter and his brother John were sentenced to be transported to America for seven years for horse stealing at Newcastle. The American War of Independence had caused transportation to be suspended until the first fleet of convict ships left for New South Wales in 1787. However the Winter brothers served the whole of their sentence on the prison hulks on the Thames and had been released on 14 August 1791, just two weeks before the murder of Margaret Crozier.

John Brown secured Winter in a house nearby and pursued and arrested the woman with two asses. She gave her name as Jane 'Douglas', she was actually using her mother's maiden name and was more correctly known as Jane Clarke. Clarke was taken to the house where Winter was held and denied that she knew him, Winter on the other hand said 'that he had been with her for some nights and that she was the only wife he then had.' Brown separated the prisoners and went into the back yard where the asses had been taken and searched the sacks on them. He found some currants and raisins and a gully knife. Meanwhile one of the other Elsdon groups searching for the suspects, led by parish constable William Nicholson, came up to the house at Horsley having heard that Winter and Clarke had been detained. With that group was the shepherd boy Robert Hindmarsh. Brown brought the prisoners together and put other men and women in the same room, creating an 18th century identification parade. Robert Hindmarsh was then shown into the room and identified William Winter and Jane Clarke as two of the three people he had seen on Whisker Shield Fell the day before the murder was discovered. He also said that Clarke was the woman who handled the knife.

John Brown's next task was to bring them before a magistrate and have them committed to prison. The justice of the peace for the Elsdon district, who became deeply involved with this case, was Walter Trevelyan (from another branch of the Trevelyan family of Wallington) who lived at Netherwitton Hall. He was then about 48 years of age. John Brown hired horses to transport the prisoners. Winter asked to stop on their way through Stamfordham to prove that he had spent the previous Monday night sleeping at the Black Bull Inn. The landlady, Mrs Jordan, said she would swear on her oath 'that neither he nor persons of any kind was lodged at that time under her roof.' Winter 'grumbled much at this.' In a confession to Walter Trevelyan later, he alleged that some of the stolen clothing, including two lawn handkerchiefs, had been sold to Mrs Jordan who knew where it had come from, and when in custody at Stamfordham he saw that 'one of the aforesaid handkerchiefs was about the neck of Jordan's daughter.'

Another significant incident took place at Stamfordham when Jane Clarke asked to stop and buy a pair of shoes, throwing away the old ones. William Nicholson, who was travelling with the escort group, 'took up the old shoes thinking they might be evidence against the man and the woman.' Back at Elsdon, Nicholson showed the shoes to the farmer, George Hedley, who made a mark in soft ground with the heel of one of the shoes and identified it as exactly the same mark he had seen at East Nook next to the 'pike of hay' and spoken of at the inquest.

Arriving eventually at Netherwitton Hall, John Brown found that Walter Trevelyan was not at home, but on Saturday 3 September another justice, Brian Mitford, committed the two prisoners to the gaol at Morpeth. Winter and Clarke admitted their true identity to Mitford. It was also recorded that Jane Clarke 'confessed in part that William Winter set off for the purpose of Robbing a house Northward.' The prisoners had begun to blame each other. They were lodged in the care of John Blake, the gaoler at the county gaol at Morpeth, and John Brown returned to Elsdon.

Meanwhile the *Newcastle Courant* carried a report of the murder in the 'GENERAL HUE AND CRY'.

MURDER AND ROBBERY Whereas late on Monday night or early on Tuesday morning last, Margaret Crozer of the Raw, Near Elsdon, in the county of Northumberland, was murdered, and the house robbed of sundry articles of Wearing Apparel, Linen Drapery &c. such as Muslins, Printed Cottons and Handkerchiefs. For the purpose of bringing the Perpetrators to Justice, the Parish Of Elsdon hereby offer a reward of FIVE POUNDS to be paid on conviction of the offendor or offenders, by the Rev. Mr. Harrison of Elsdon. Two women and a man of very suspicious appearance were seen lurking near the house the preceding day and were met the next day with an ass laden, near to Harlow Hill. The man was about six feet high, black hair tied back in a club behind, had on a light coloured coat, light blue breeches, and grey stockings. The women were very tall and stout, one of them particularly so, they were both dressed in grey cloaks, black bonnets, and one of them wore a light stamped cotton gown.'

Newcastle Courant Saturday 3 September 1791

Another vestry meeting was held at St Cuthbert's Church Elsdon on Sunday 4 September 1791. John Brown and two others set out again the next day and, following up on information they had gathered earlier, crossed south over the River Tyne. They arrested the second woman seen by the shepherd boys, Eleanor Clarke (or Douglas), sister to the first woman in custody, at Medomsley. They also arrested Jane Clarke (or Douglas) mother of the two sisters. Mother and daughter were wearing items of clothing stolen from the Raw and the constables recovered other stolen items.

John Brown hired two horses at Medomsley to transport the prisoners and the stolen goods and travelled to Netherwitton via Hunt Law near Black Heddon to check an alibi for Jane Clarke (the mother). Witnesses confirmed that the mother had spent the night of the murder at Hunt Law but her daughters were not with her.

Brown and his group brought the new prisoners before Walter Trevelyan at Netherwitton Hall on the evening of the same day. Over the following days, steady progress was made by Walter Trevelyan examining witnesses and taking their depositions. The justice of the peace of the 18th century had a more active investigative role than a 20th century magistrate. The women gave no formal written information. They were examined by the

Netherwitton Hall, built in 1685.

magistrate about the contents of the sack of goods found in their possession. Jane Clarke (the mother) told Trevelyan 'that they were such things as they used, that they were their own, that they were honestly come by and could be accounted for.' However Trevelyan pieced together positive identifications of goods in the possession of the prisoners as being specially made by Mary Temple and various other witnesses and stolen from Margaret Crozier. The stolen clothing included a cap worn by Jane Clarke and a petticoat worn by her sister Eleanor and six caps recovered from Jane Clarke (the mother). The net was closing around the prisoners.

The examination of William Winter by Walter Trevelyan and his fellow justice Brian Mitford had dramatic results. Amongst the furniture at Netherwitton Hall there is still a wing-backed chair known as Winter's Chair, and family tradition has is that William Winter sat in that particular chair when examined by Walter Trevelyan. On Wednesday and Thursday 14 and 15 September 1791, William Winter made a long and detailed written 'Voluntary Examination and Confession' (Public Record Office Access No. ASSI 45/37/3/225) to the magistrates setting out his account of the events at the Raw.

Winter confessed to taking a leading role in the burglary but denied any part in the murder, laying the blame on the two girls. After his release from the prison hulks on the

his
William ✗ Winter
Mark

Thames in August 1791, Winter quickly made his way to Northumberland and joined up with the Clarke family. He was in desperate need of money and Jane Clarke (the mother) told him she had 'been in the house of a woman at the Raw and that they had bought a half quarter of tobacco and that they had seen about £50 worth of goods lying upon her table', and her daughters would go and show him where it was …' Winter and the two Clarke sisters took an ass and set off north to the Raw by way of Black Heddon, Little Harle, Kirk Whelpington, crossing the turnpike road near Elsdon to Whisker Shield – a route that passed the very spot where the body of William Winter was to be gibbeted some 12 months later.

Winter agreed that they had encountered the shepherd boys on Whisker Shield Common or Fell, when the gang stopped to take refreshments. They went on from there to a place near the Raw and waited until very late at night when all the lights had gone out. (This was the place where next morning the farmer, George Hedley, found the marks of Jane Clarke's shoes.) At the pele Winter slipped the wooden bar holding the door in place. They went into Crozier's home and the Clarke sisters 'went to the bed to keep the woman quiet & to prevent her from making a noise, the Woman then being awake, that the women then went into the Bed where the Woman was lying & got one each side of her where they remained while he opened three locks on two chests and a cupboard.' Winter said he warned the Clarkes not to hurt Crozier and he gathered together numerous pieces of clothing handkerchiefs, shawls etc., and quantities of currants and raisins and some bread and cheese. He left the house to pack and hide the stolen goods in an oatfield nearby.

Winter soon returned and urged the women to leave and after they had left the house he returned alone to the bedside, touched Margaret Crozier and found she did not stir; he shook her, then lit a candle and found that 'her handkerchief was drawn very tight around her neck and tied very tight with two knots, that he untied the handkerchief and threw some cold water upon her face, that he found that she would not come to life, that she was dead.'

Winter laid her down and left the house to join his accomplices. When they reached the oatfield where he had deposited the goods he: 'said to the two women lasses you have done a very bad action I dare say the old woman will never speak anymore, and they replied that they had tied her up by her meat meaning they had hanged her.'

They loaded the stolen goods on the ass and set off for Kirk Whelpington but got lost and settled down by 'a hayhile' (hay rick) until daylight. They ate the bread and cheese and fed the ass on green peas stolen from the house of Margaret Crozier. Winter also confirmed 'the Clarks had a gulley with them … he asked Eleanor Clarke what had become of the Gulley she said that it was left in the Bed.' They set off for Kirk Whelpington at daylight. Winter saw that Jane Clarke was now wearing a pair of blue coarse woollen stockings instead of the black stockings she wore going to the house at the Raw, 'he bid her put them off as she might lose her life by them & that she replied she did not care, on which he replied that she might do as she pleased.'

They met up with Jane Clarke (the mother) at Huntlaw as previously arranged about eleven o'clock on the Tuesday morning. They examined and sorted the stolen goods and it was then, according to Winter, that Jane Clarke (the mother) went off to Stamfordham and sold goods to Mrs Jordan at the Black Bull Inn, consisting of 15 yards of blue Shalloon (light woollen stuff for linings), handkerchiefs and some cambric for 30 shillings. Jordan 'knew the same were stolen and where they came from.' They travelled south together and crossed the Tyne at 'Wylam Boats' on Wednesday night. The following day Jane Clarke (the mother) told Winter 'Jordan wanted a dozen cheeses & a butter furkin or two if he could get them'. Jane Clarke (the daughter) and Winter crossed the Tyne again, stealing a fleece and some wooden bowls from a house near Acomb later in the day and reaching Horsley Moor on Friday morning only to be 'apprehended by eleven persons!'

Many points of detail in Winter's account dovetailed in with what the witnesses had said, but there were notable exceptions. The handkerchief had not been untied from Crozier's neck and the story of Winter attempting to resuscitate Crozier did not match up with what Barbara Drummond discovered the morning after the murder. This brings into question Winter's attempt to distance himself from the death of Margaret Crozier.

Interesting details emerge of how this investigation was financed. Because the criminals were found, the expenses incurred did not fall on the parish but were authorised by the Quarter Sessions to be paid by the county treasurer. So John Brown's expenses were met but his loss of earnings or income through absence from his farm was not refunded, so a heavy burden fell on the resourceful Northumbrian who held the unpaid parish appointment.

Winter and the three Clarke women were held in the county gaol in Bridge Street, Morpeth, to face trial for the murder of Margaret Crozier, burglary at the Raw and receiving stolen goods. These serious charges, carrying the death penalty, could only be tried at the Northumberland Assizes that were held at Newcastle upon Tyne about the beginning of August each year. The Winter Gang, having missed the 1791 sitting of the assizes, faced a long wait in prison until August 1792.

During that year Winter was joined by other prisoners charged with capital crimes. They included William Gardener, committed to prison on 20 June 1792 charged with stealing sheep. Gardner was given a macabre role to play at the end of this affair.

It was a harsh cold winter; the Tyne was frozen over for a long period around Christmas and people passed freely across the ice between Newcastle and Gateshead. The shipping trade was at a standstill causing great hardship for those who relied on the water for their livelihood.

On Saturday 4 August 1792, the long wait was over for Winter and the others. The gentlemen of town and county gathered to go with the High Sheriff of Northumberland to meet the judges at the Gateshead boundary and escort them safely to Newcastle upon Tyne. Then followed the annual pomp and ceremony at the Guildhall and the old Moot Hall to open the Assizes, the escort of the judges to their residence at the Mansion House on the Quayside and, on the Sunday, a public procession to a grand service at St Nicholas Church, which the population of the town turned out to see.

Meanwhile John Blake, the county gaoler at Morpeth, had moved William Winter, the Clarkes and the other county prisoner awaiting trial to the dungeon of the Keep at Newcastle, where they were held heavily ironed in great discomfort and exposed to the weather because of the poor condition of the roof of the building. Payments recorded in the Northumberland Quarter Sessions records show that a woman named Ann Hardie 'Keeper of the Moot Hall' was paid 'fourteen shillings for cleaning the Great Hall and Gaol at the Castle of Newcastle upon Tyne and for finding straw for the prisoners.'

The trial of Winter and the three women was fixed for Wednesday 8

The Tyne Bridge (rebuilt after the floods of 1771), the Castle Keep and the Moot Hall beside it in 1807.

August 1792 before Baron Thompson, who had presided over other trials of the Faws. As it was a Northumberland crime it was tried at Castlegarth in the Moot Hall. Winter, the Clarke sisters and their mother were jointly charged with murdering Margaret Crozier 'by divers mortal bruises and fractures', the indictment document, which is preserved at the Public Record Office, asserting that they:

> feloniously, wilfully and of their malice aforethought did choak and strangle, of which said several mortal bruises and Fractures, Choaking and Strangling the said Margaret Crozier then and there instantly died.

(Public Record Office Access No. ASSI 44/107/Part 1)

The whole of that indictment is an interesting example of 18th century legal language. There was a further indictment against Winter and the two young women of burglary at Margaret Crozier's home. Jane Clarke, the mother, was also charged with receiving goods stolen from Margaret Crozier. The Grand Jury for Northumberland, a group of 24 gentlemen of the county, with Sir William Middleton of Belsay as Foreman, considered the charges against the Winter Gang and then endorsed the indictments 'A

True Bill' thereby approving the case going forward for a full trial. There were two dozen prosecution witnesses in what became a marathon one-day hearing. The court records show that the court sitting began at 7.30am and ended at 11.30pm, some 16 hours of continuous business.

The petty jury found William Winter and the sisters Jane and Eleanor Clarke guilty of murder and burglary. Jane Clarke 'the Elder' was cleared of all charges. It was, therefore, very late at night when Baron Thompson passed sentence on Winter and the Clarke sisters. Eighteenth century law required the judge to sentence persons convicted of murder to death by hanging followed either by dissection of their bodies by the surgeons or gibbeting at a place near to the scene of their crime. The court record in this case is endorsed:

Northern Circuit Minute Book 1789-1810

Guilty Murder – To be Hanged on Friday next and their Bodies to be afterwards dissected and Anatomized'.

(Public Record Office Access No. ASSI 42/12)

Winter and the Clarke sisters were returned to the dungeon at the Keep, and, in accordance with the same law, held in solitary confinement, fed on bread and water, except for receiving the holy sacrament, and executed on the next day but one after sentence. That next day the judge Baron Thompson cancelled the instruction for the body of William Winter to be dissected and anatomised and made an order that Winter's body:

Northern Circuit Minute Book 1789-1810

Shall be hung in chains on some conspicuous part of Whiskershiel Common at a distance of one hundred yards from the Turnpike Road leading to Elsdon.

(Public Record Office Access No. ASSI 42/12)

Arrangements were made for the executions to be carried out on the county gallows outside the West Gate in the Newcastle town walls. At the same Northumberland Assizes, William Gardner was convicted of sheep stealing and sentenced to death by hanging. Gardner agreed to be the executioner of Winter and the Clarke sisters and for taking on that office Baron Thompson reprieved his death sentence and substituted transportation to New South Wales for seven years.

On Friday morning 10 August 1792, William Winter, Jane Clarke and Eleanor Clarke were taken out of the dungeon at the Keep, put into a cart and were drawn to the West Gate in a procession led by a clergyman and scholars singing psalms. The traditional route from the Keep to the county gallows was to leave Castlegarth by the Black Gate across into Back Row, a narrow street formerly called Gallowgate, then by way of Westgate Street through the West Gate, across Skinnerburn to the County of Northumberland and the gallows. According to the *Newcastle Advertizer* report, the crowds were so great that hundreds of people were unable to make their way through the West Gate to watch the execution.

It was about eleven o'clock when the procession reached the West Gate. The clergyman entered the cart and spent a long time in prayer with Winter and the two women. William Winter then made a speech admitting his guilt of the crime and forgiving those who had given evidence against him. The women had nothing to say before execution.

The report in the *Advertizer* then described the final moments:

> The clergyman then took leave of them, the two women embraced each other and the executioner having tied the ropes, they were all launched into eternity together. William Winter appeared to be about 40 years of age; the two women who were sisters appeared under twenty. They behaved very penitently and met their fate with great fortitude neither of the women having shed a single tear during the whole of their being under the gallows.

The *Newcastle Courant* report on this execution included a compliment to the magistrate Walter Trevelyan:

> Much praise is due to the worthy magistrate who with such laudable zeal interested himself in bringing to condign punishment these perpetrators of this barbarous deed. The Country has on many occasions experienced the good effects of his endeavours to extirpate the nefarious gang of strollers which have so long infested the County of Northumberland.
>
> *Newcastle Courant* Saturday 11 August 1792

When he died on 12 June 1819, aged 78, Walter Trevelyan was described in the same newspaper as 'a most active and efficient magistrate, and greatly esteemed in private life.'

The custom was to leave the bodies hanging for about an hour on the gallows at the West Gate before cutting them down. The bodies of the two Clarke sisters were delivered to the Barber Surgeons Hall at Manors. The practice was for the surgeons to dissect and anatomise the bodies of executed criminals in public while giving lectures on anatomy.

Winter's body was taken out to the turnpike road to the south of Elsdon in accordance with the orders of the judge. Special lifting tackle was required to place the body on the gibbet near Steng Cross in sight of Whiskershiel Common where William Winter had encountered the shepherd boys 12 months earlier. The costs for the gibbet amounted to £12 9s 10d.

Winter's Gibbet, or Winter's Stob as it is sometimes called, became a famous landmark and features on all subsequent maps of the district. The beams of gibbets were liberally covered with sharp spikes to prevent anyone climbing up to remove the body or interfere with it. Gibbeted bodies were left hanging in place indefinitely as a grim warning until they disappeared by natural process. In time Winter's Gibbet decayed, in some part due to the country practice of taking pieces of the gibbet to chew or rub on their teeth as a cure for toothache. The gibbet was replaced on several occasions. Writing some 30 years after the execution, Eneas Mackenzie in his *History of Northumberland* (1822), said: 'This loathsome spectacle [i.e. Winter's Gibbet] at length fell into pieces and another gibbet, on which the rude figure of a man is suspended, occupies its place.' This is the first reference to wooden effigies on the gibbet. It is said that men would shoot at the wooden effigy for sport. Gradually it disintegrated leaving only the wooden head.

In about 1867, Sir Walter Trevelyan of Wallington Hall ordered that a replica gibbet should be put up on the site. The local legend, which persists amongst residents there to this day, is that the replica gibbet was erected on Wallington land on a different spot to the original. There is strong support for this belief because the first Ordnance Survey map of the area, made in 1859, shows the site of the remains of the gibbet in that year within the Parish of Elsdon about 40 to 50 yards south west of the present site. Winter's Gibbet now stands a yard or two inside the Parish of Hartburn and within Wallington land.

Stories abound of creaking chains and the stench from the gibbet alarming passing travellers. It is said that it became necessary to draw the rotting remains of Winter's body into a sack and eventually shepherds buried the remnants somewhere nearby. Patricia Jennings of the Trevelyan family has written of damage to the gibbet and to the wooden heads, carved by Robin Dower, that have been suspended from the gibbet in recent times. The heads have frequently been stolen and a fibreglass cast was made to help with the problem of replacement. The practice of gibbeting the bodies of some executed criminals ended in 1834.

The Winter family and their associates had other fatal experience of justice as will be seen later. Given this background it is hardly surprising that the broadsheet published at Newcastle upon Tyne following the execution of William Winter and the Clarke sisters began with the paragraph quoted at the opening of this chapter.

It seems probable that the broadsheet was drafted for the printer or entirely written by one of the clergymen attending Winter and the others in the dungeon at the Keep at Newcastle and at their execution. This was common practice, evidenced by the expressive language attributed to Winter, who was, after all, an illiterate uneducated man: 'I really and truly repent of the crime of which I am convicted, of which I acknowledge myself, with sorrow, guilty, and may the Divine Power to whom I with humility look up for mercy, forgive and protect me.'

In the broadsheet there is an interesting reference to his brother John who had been with William Winter on the prison hulks on the Thames. They separated before the murder of Margaret Crozier, 'But I have received but indifferent usage from my friends, and am much surprised that my brother John should come to aggravate my misfortunes at this dungeon window.' There is a small window at the dungeon of the Keep at Newcastle. What happened at the 'dungeon window' is now lost in time, but the Northumberland Quarter Sessions records show that the authorities were quick to deal with John Winter following the execution of his brother. John Winter was found to be a 'rogue and vagabond' and committed to the house of correction for a spell, then sent to be 'employed in His Majesty's Service by sea.' By the end of the century John Winter had not only deserted from the navy but was held in the County Gaol at Morpeth as a deserter from the army. He escaped from the gaol in March 1800 and was not heard of again.

A rear view of the old gaol at Morpeth in 1993. It closed as a gaol in 1828.

A number of myths and legends have grown up around the Winter case over the past 200 years. For example one of the more enduring myths is that Margaret Crozier died of having her throat cut, whereas the poor woman actually died of strangulation and a fracture of the left temple after a severe beating.

Another interesting legend concerns the action of the shepherd boys. There can be little doubt after reading the depositions that the two shepherd boys played a pivotal role in bringing the Winter Gang to the notice of the authorities and eventually to justice. The depositions make it clear that of the two boys involved, Hindmarsh and Best, the key evidence of identification and so on, came from Robert Hindmarsh. It was Hindmarsh who reported to his master Abraham Southern what they had seen and it was Hindmarsh who was taken out with the search parties after the murder and identified Winter and Jane Clarke at Horsley.

Over the past 200 years writers came to focus on Robert Hindmarsh and a story about the boy identifying a pattern of nails in boots worn by William Winter. There is nothing to support this tale in the depositions of Hindmarsh, Best nor anyone else, nor in any record contemporary to the arrest, investigation and trial. The story about the boot nails first appears in 1827 (*History of Northumberland*, John Hodgson) and then is much developed and embellished by later writers. The weakness of this legend is that the shepherd boys never saw the soles of William Winter's boots, he was standing up all time on Whisker Shield Common; secondly no such boot marks were found by any witness and thirdly, Winter had changed his shoes before being arrested. If such evidence had been available the parish constables and Walter Trevelyan would have taken the same care with it as they had with the evidence about Jane Clarke's shoes.

Baden Powell, the famous Scout pioneer, was impressed by this legend about the shepherd boys and used it in his book *Scouting for Boys* as an example of good observation, citizenship and other laudable qualities. Through the Scout movement the tale of Winter's Gibbet has circulated around the world. The shepherd lad Hindmarsh deserved all those plaudits but for different reasons. He should also be remembered as a brave young boy because in the time after the trial he is said to have been threatened and molested by associates of the Winter Gang. According to local parish records he died at only 20 years of age on 14 November 1800.

The parish constable, John Brown, was faced with a major murder enquiry in this remote place. He was a farmer, untrained and unprepared for this demand on him, but this shrewd Northumbrian faced the challenge with courage, common sense and determination. Better days lay ahead for him. On 19 May 1795, at Elsdon Parish Church, John Brown married his cousin Elizabeth Jackson who, with Barbara Drummond, had discovered the body of Margaret Crozier. They lived at the Raw and had six children.

The handcuffs belonging to parish constable John Brown of Elsdon.

Barry Redfern

John Brown died on 4 May 1827 aged 73 and was buried in Elsdon churchyard. His gravestone can be seen there to this day. Margaret Crozier's grave in the same churchyard is not marked. Descendants of the Brown family still live in Northumberland and one of them has possession of the handcuffs used by John Brown in his duties as parish constable of Elsdon.

Neither headstone nor public memorial remains to Margaret Crozier but back at the pele tower at the Raw there is a single window high up on the east-facing wall and enclosed now by a barn. Carved in stone to the right of the window are the head and shoulders of a woman and, to the left, the outline of a chair. How the carvings came to be put there is not known, but the local legend is that the woman's image is Margaret Crozier and the chair is the one she used in her home at the Raw.

William Winter and Jane and Eleanor Clarke were members of a loose-knit gang of violent criminal tinkers known as the Faw Gang or the Faas who terrorised Northumberland in the 18th century, travelling about stealing and breaking into property at will.

Barry Redfern

The two carvings at the Raw can just be made out here. On the right is the head and shoulders of a womsn, and on the left, the outline of a chair.

5. The Faw Gangs

The decision of the justices at the Northumberland Quarter Sessions at Morpeth in the Spring of 1752 to offer a special reward for the arrest and conviction of the people known as Faws gives some indication of the problem.

The word Faws or Faas is said to be a corruption of the name Fall and was applied to a wandering fraternity of gypsy folk loosely linked by blood and kinship. Their activities in the 18th century were not, as will be seen, confined to Northumberland and the borders, but they were a great source of trouble for the authorities and fear for communities in those districts at that time. The Faws were thought to have their ancient roots in Egypt. One of their leaders in the borders in the 16th century was known as Johnny Faa the Lord and Earl of Little Egypt, and in the same century people could be hanged simply for being gypsies or 'Egyptians'. All of which may account for a strange entry in the burial registers of St Nicholas Parish Church, Durham, 8 August 1592: 'Simson, Arrington, Fetherstone, Fenwicke and Lancaster – hanged for being Egyptians.'

The Faws lived by their wits. They made and sold brooms, mended pots and pans, dealt in eggs, poultry, clothing, earthenware and anything else they could lay their hands on. The women would tell fortunes and use any amount of trickery on gullible and superstitious people. For example in February 1751/2 the local newspapers reported that the Faws were active in and around Durham City, stealing hay, poultry and whatever else they could lay their hands on during the night. One of the Faw women went into the servants' quarters of a gentleman's house on a Saturday morning, claiming that she could tell the fortune of anyone who would put a piece of gold into her hand. One credulous woman did just that and, pretending she needed to go to the door to strengthen her clairvoyant powers, the fortune teller made off with the guinea she had been given. She was soon caught, however and sent to prison. The newspaper ended its report with this rather pious sentiment:

> **This ought to caution all such to distrust their Credulity, and, for the future, to wait patiently the Decree of Providence.**

Newcastle Courant Saturday 1 February 1751/1752

Another of trick of the fortune tellers was to work in pairs. pretending to be dumb but having special powers because of that disability. A short spell at hard labour in the House of Correction would bring about a remarkable recovery of the power of speech as reported in the Tyneside newspapers:

> **On Saturday last Mary and Ann Stewart were committed to the Tower on the Bridge for Telling of Fortunes by Signs pretending to be dumb; and Tuesday they were sent to the Workhouse for a Month, where they (through the good Effects of hard labour) in a few Hours found the Use of their Tongues.**

Newcastle Journal 28 March 1752

The 'Tower on the Bridge' was a small prison on the old stone bridge across the Tyne at Newcastle. It was used as an overnight lock-up for prisoners being held to appear before the justices of the peace. That bridge was swept away in the great floods of 1771. The Tower on the Bridge gaol was replaced by another lock-up in the Close.

The account of the Winter case has demonstrated in a vivid fashion that the Faw women would go further than telling fortunes and were quite prepared to become personally involved in the dirty business of murder, burglary and the disposal of stolen property. The Winter family and their associates in the Faw Gang had other fatal experiences of justice apart from the murder of Margaret Crozier. William Winter had a brother, John Winter, whose criminal career has been described earlier. There were at least two more brothers. Tom Winter changed his name to Tom Spring and moved away from the North East. He achieved some fame as a pugilist and is said to have died in about 1852 as a respected tavern keeper in London. The fourth brother was called Robert Winter. The father of the four brothers, another John Winter, was a man familiar with the gaols in the North East. He was, for example, held in the county gaol at Morpeth as early as 1752 as a vagrant, but his final and fatal brush with the law came in 1788 committing crimes along the North Tyne.

Again it was the columns of the 'GENERAL HUE AND CRY' in the *Newcastle Courant* that alerted the public to the activities of the Winter family. This time they attacked the home of the famous border family, the Charltons of Hesleyside. About one o'clock on Monday morning 4 February 1788 John Winter, his son Robert and two other Faws, John Clark and Alexander Drummond, broke into the Charlton mansion and made off with a tankard and a mass of household linen. How they entered the house is not known, but this practice of waiting until depth of the night to break into houses appears to have been common amongst the Faws. The murder of Margaret Crozier took place the same way, and other examples will follow.

The publicity in the Hue and Cry does not mention it, but this gang of Faws actually committed two burglaries that day. Winter and the other Faws made their way from Hesleyside some six miles or so south east to Birtley in the North Tyne and, at about eight o'clock in the evening, broke into the home of William Hogg, stealing shirts and other things. Such goods were attractive to the Faws as they were easily disposed of at the isolated hamlets and villages they passed through in their nomadic life style. In fact the frequent movement of these people around the borders, despite the obstacles to 18th century travel, is one of the more interesting features of the way they lived.

There followed a will-o-the-wisp chase of the gang around the borders. Reports in the Hue and Cry columns passed on to the public their descriptions and the latest sightings including:

Travelling 'all the bye roads' is an apt way to describe the twisting and turning of this group of Faws with the shadow of the gallows following them about the borders as they had committed several capital crimes. They would be well aware of the intense enquiries afoot to trace them. In the space of a little over a month they had been in Hesleyside, Birtley, St John Lee, Cambo, Clennel, Kale Water, Jedburgh, Yetholm, and Selkirk. However the next week, 22 March 1788, saw the announcement of the arrest of one the Faws. John Clark was arrested and detained in the House of Correction at Morpeth as an 'Idle and Disorderly Person' pending investigation of numerous crimes.

> Any person or persons desirous of bringing the said John Clark to justice for any crime by him committed, may have an opportunity of seeing and examining him, by applying to the Keeper of the House of Correction aforesaid.
>
> *Newcastle Courant* Saturday 22 March 1788

Some time elapsed before the ring leader was tracked down. It was on 7 June 1788 that the *Courant* announced that 'Old Winter' had been arrested at Lanark and was now confined in the county gaol at Morpeth. The magistrate, Walter Trevelyan of Netherwitton, that robust defender of Northumberland against the Faws, sent John Blake, the county gaoler at Morpeth, and his assistants to bring Winter back to the county for trial. The

Winter family and John Clark were charged with the burglaries at Hesleyside and Birtley and held in the county gaol at Morpeth to await their trial at the Assizes at Newcastle upon Tyne.

'Old Winter' and his associates appeared before the Judge, Sir Alexander Thompson, at the Northumberland Assizes Old Moot Hall in Castlegarth Newcastle on Tuesday 22 July 1788. No detailed account of their trials has survived, but it is recorded that John Clark turned King's Evidence, that is to say gave evidence for the Crown against his criminal partners, and thereby saved his own life. John and Robert Winter, father and son were convicted of the burglaries and horse stealing and were sentenced to death by hanging. Margaret Winter was cleared of her charges but ordered to remain in gaol.

The prisoners were held in the county gaol at Bridge Street in Morpeth until the capital sentence was carried out at Fair Moor outside Morpeth on Wednesday 6 August 1788.

On Wednesday last John and Robert Winter, the father and son, were executed at Morpeth pursuant to their sentence for breaking open the house of William Charlton Esq., of Heslieside; as they had lived for many years in the course of the most daring and shameless villainy, at their death they testified the most brutal want of feeling, fear or compunction. We understand these wretches formed part of a numerous gang, many of whom are equally notorious, and doubtless merit a similar punishment.

Newcastle Chronicle Saturday 9 August 1788

The *Newcastle Courant*, on the other hand, carried a report that Robert Winter had made a speech expressing regret that the manner of his upbringing and the way he lived had brought him to this ignominious and untimely end and he warned all the young people present against following his example. The same newspaper carried a timely crime prevention warning to the public in anticipation of the Newcastle Fair on 12 August. It warned that fairs were a magnet for 'Pick-pockets, Booth-thieves, Shop-lifters, Sharpers, Swindlers &c.' and cautioned the people to be 'suspicious of every stranger with whom they deal.' Finally it exhorted readers to:

A significant Faws name appeared in the list of prisoners at the
Northumberland Assizes in July 1788 – Walter Clarke, charged with stealing
eight stone of wool at Doddington in Northumberland. Clarke was not
convicted on this occasion but this is the man who was the father of Jane
and Eleanor Clarke, hanged in 1792 with William Winter for the murder of
Margaret Crozier.

Walter Clarke next comes to notice in 1793, 12 months after the
execution of his daughters, when he appeared at the Northumberland
Assizes again at the Old Moot Hall in Castle Garth at Newcastle with two
women, Jane Trotter and Isabel Robson, charged with burglaries at the
house of William Mills at Wooler (at about one o'clock in the morning) and
being in possession of goods stolen at Coldstream.

Another Faws prisoner of special interest appeared at the same assizes,
Margaret Dunn (or Cockburn), wife of Thomas Dunn, charged with
burglary at the house of John and Mary Somerbell at Corbridge (again
about one o'clock in the morning) and stealing money, linen and clothing.
The text of the burglary indictments again reveals that common practice of
the Faws of breaking into dwelling houses in the dead of night.

Margaret Dunn had only been in custody for ten days or so. Eighteenth
century justice on this occasion moved swiftly from crime to the ultimate
punishment of death by hanging in about five weeks. The misfortune of
these representatives of the Faw Gang was to appear before a judge with
deep knowledge of their criminal activities, 'the Honourable Sir Alexander
Thompson Knight, one of the Barons of our said Lord the King of his Court
of Exchequer'. Baron Thompson had John and Robert Winter and Walter
Clarke before him in 1788, and it was the same judge who had sentenced to
death William Winter and Clarke's daughters in 1792.

At the Northumberland Assizes on Wednesday 31 July 1793, Walter
Clarke and Isabel Robson were convicted of the burglaries and both

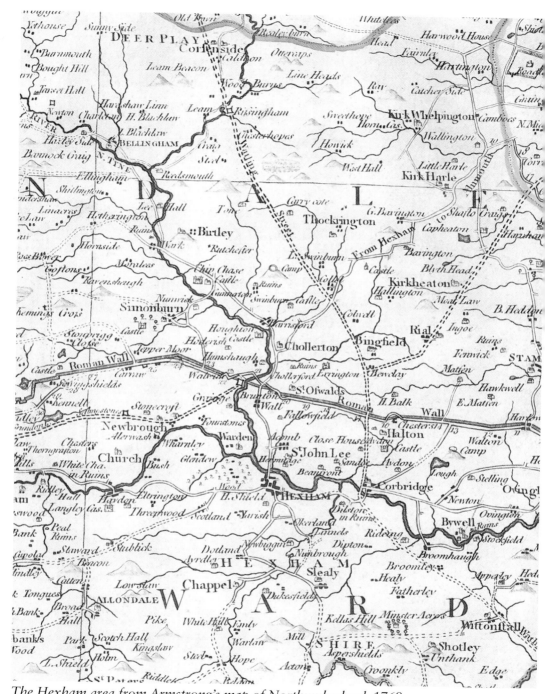

The Hexham area from Armstrong's map of Northumberland, 1769.

sentenced to be hanged. Jane Trotter was convicted of grand larceny and sentenced 'to be transported beyond the seas for seven years'. Margaret Dunn was found guilty of the burglary at Corbridge and also sentenced to be hanged. Before the Judge left town he reprieved Isabel Robson for transportation.

John Blake, the gaoler, took the prisoners back to the County Gaol at Bridge Street in Morpeth. Isabel Robson, together with a highway robber Robert Musgrave, having been reprieved by the judges, were destined to be confined in gaol at Morpeth for a further twelve months until sentence of transportation was imposed at the Assizes in 1794.

Preparations were made for Walter Clarke and Margaret Dunn to be hanged in a double execution at Fair Moor, Morpeth at the same location where John and Robert Winter, father and son were hanged in 1788.

> **Wednesday [i.e. 14 August] Walter Clarke and Margaret Dunn were executed on Fair Moor near to Morpeth, pursuant to their sentences at the last assizes for burglaries. Clarke at the fatal tree and during his confinement, behaved with great penitence, acknowledged his guilt, implored the prayers of the good and virtuous; and admonished the wicked to take warning by his untimely end, but refused to give any account of his practices, or of the gang of the Winters, with whom it is supposed he was connected, except that he was father of the two unhappy girls* who suffered with one of them last year! Margaret Dunn denied to the last that she committed the crime, for which she was about to suffer, and asserted that she fell victim to the crime of another woman, although convicted on the clearest evidence.**
>
> *Newcastle Courant* Saturday 17 August 1793
> (* i.e. Jane and Eleanor Clarke)

A copy of the execution broadsheet for Clarke and Dunn published at Newcastle upon Tyne is held in the Heritage collection at Newcastle City Library. Clarke was said to be about 50 years of age and Dunn was described as a notorious offender about 45 years of age and 'shewed some

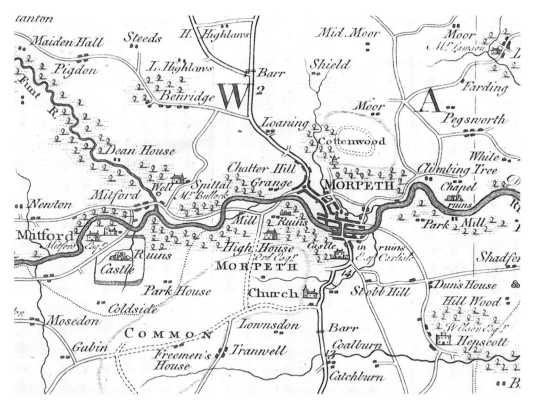

The Morpeth area from Armstrong's map, 1769.

faint sign of contrition at least'. In August 1766 as a young woman of 25 years or so, she had appeared at the Newcastle Assizes charged with forgery of a promissory note. She was sentenced to death but reprieved. At the next Assizes in 1767, she was sentenced to be transported for 14 years. By 1793 Dunn was married or co-habiting with Thomas Dunn, a soldier in the North Yorks Regiment of Militia and stationed at Newcastle upon Tyne in August of that year. She had followed her husband north from Yorkshire with the militia. He deserted after the burglary committed by his wife and, according to her account in the broadsheet, took the stolen money with him.

The broadsheet also mentions a nephew of Margaret Dunn named William Cockburn. His journey to the gallows began with another of the entries in the Hue and Cry, this time about horse-stealing at Whittingham:

GENERAL HUE AND CRY

Whittingham 23rd March 1785 STOLEN

From Thrunton in the Parish of Whittingham and county of Northumberland, on Monday night the 21st inst., or early on Tuesday morning following:

TWO MARES, one the property of Robert Whitham; she is a bright bay mare, about fifteen hands high, a remarkable long head, wide eared, a bald face, both forelegs and far hind foot white, a switch tail and with foal. The other, a black Mare, belonging to James Gibson, about fourteen hands and a half high, a bald face and far hind foot white, a thin switch tail, a stroke upon the far fore shoulder not yet haired, and a remarkable swirle upon her far hind hip.

Newcastle Courant, Saturday 26 March 1785

The report goes on to say that two suspicious men had been seen loitering about Whittingham that evening. They were seen in a public house well after 10pm, but left very suddenly. One of them was about five feet nine inches tall, thin and dark with a long neck. He was wearing a claret coloured great coat, a blue strait coat and three waistcoats (the upper one was red). The other man was about five feet six inches tall, with a full face and a roman nose. He was also wearing a claret coloured great coat, with a pair of corduroy breeches. The Association of Whittingham offered a ten-guinea reward for their arrest.

One of these suspects was William Cockburn who, with his wife, was arrested at York in April 1785. They were transferred north to the county gaol at Morpeth into the care of John Kent, the keeper of the gaol at that time. Cockburn and his wife were brought before the Northumberland Assizes at the Moot Hall in Newcastle on Monday 25 July 1785. William Cockburn was convicted of stealing the horses at Whittingham in March, but his wife was cleared and discharged. Four persons were sentenced to death at the Northumberland Assizes that month, William Cockburn for horse stealing, William Graham for house breaking, William Davison for sheep stealing and James Wintrup, alias Winter, for horse stealing, Davison and Wintrup were reprieved for transportation but Cockburn and Graham, the housebreaker, were, as the newspapers of the time were apt to say, 'left by the judges for execution.' Wintrup, alias Winter, may have been a member of the Winter family in the Faws Gang, as it was said that some of the Winters adopted the name Wintrup to try to avoid the notoriety of the family name. Cockburn and Graham spent the last days of their lives in the county gaol at Morpeth and on Tuesday 16 August 1785 they were executed on Fair Moor near Morpeth.

When the records of these executions are put together with those of the Winter gang, an extraordinary Northumberland Gallows Family Tree emerges (see page 4). Eight members of the Faws, closely related or associated, were hanged on the county gallows at Morpeth and Newcastle upon Tyne in the space of eight years.

Early 18th century records, dating from the reign of Queen Anne, reveal that these people were also known as Baileys, Shaws and ffalls alias ffawes and the Northumberland authorities were experiencing great problems with them. The justices meeting at Alnwick in 1711 were alarmed at the conduct of the Faws in the county and offered rewards for their arrest as vagabonds.

Northumberland Quarter Sessions Order Book 1710 – 1719

Michaelmass Sessions 3rd October 1711 at Alnwicke.

Baileys als Faws. Whereas several notorious vagrants calling themselves by the names Baileys, Shaws, ffalls als ffawes have of late come into this county and keep themselves together in several parts thereof threatening to burn houses and are suspected of burglaries and other evil practices and ride armed to the great terror of Her Majestys subjects. It is ordered by the court with the seale of this court a warrant issue forth to take and apprehend the vagrants and bring them before some of Her Majestys Justices for this County that they may be proceeded against and dealt with according to law.

(Northumberland Record Office Access No. QSO 5)

A reward of £5 was offered to anyone who arrested a member of one of these families (over the age of 16) and brought them before the county magistrates.

At an adjourned sessions, in October 1711, John and Leonard Hunter were paid £50 for apprehending 'above tenn men and women of the aforesaid gang or company of ffawes who are now in custody in Morpeth

Gaole.' The justices decided to seek an order to transport them. This anxiety about the behaviour of the Faws was to prove only too well founded. The authorities were to experience much difficulty with this particular gang of Faws. At the next sessions the prisoners, still not formally named in official records, were remanded on as 'Incorrigible Rogues' whilst the justices sought authority to transport them out of the country.

Six months or so later, the Faws had been transferred to the gaol in Newcastle Keep and special precautions had to be taken because it was suspected that their accomplices were planning to help these prisoners escape. But despite the extra security some of the Faws did break

out of the gaol at Castlegarth and damaged the building in doing so. The blame for the escape was laid squarely on George Grey, the Keeper of the Moot Hall and Castle Gaol.

> **At the Midsummer Sessions 16th August 1712 at Hexham, Grey was deprived of his salary and ordered to return his keys to the Sheriff. As several suspicious people had been seen lurking near the gaol at night (presumably with the intent of helping prisoners to escape), a warrant was issued to arrest anyone found doing so.**

(Northumberland Record Office Access No. QSO 5, pages 104 & 97)

The authorities also incurred continuous heavy expense for watching the prisoners, fitting new irons and locks, feeding and maintaining the 'ffourteen of the ffawes' in the gaol up to the time of the escape. At the sessions in October 1712 (12 months after the start of their problems with the Faws) payments of £46 8s 0d. were authorised to repair the 'Castle Prison,' so significant damage had been caused to the building during the escape. The justices also ordered that the Faws women and children held under special watch at the Castle Prison be transferred to Morpeth Gaol. It would appear therefore that the adult male Faws escaped from the gaol leaving most of the women and children behind. In the records of the next sessions held at

Morpeth in January 1712/13, there is a list of names of these Faws including, Bailey, Addison, Carr and Hornsby, together with an order for the women remaining in gaol to be whipped through Morpeth.

Northumberland Quarter Sessions Order Book 1710 – 1719

Christmas Sessions, 14 January 1712/13 at Morpeth

Fawes or Baileys. Ordered that the four women now in Gaole be whipped next Market Day through the Towne of Morpeth and dismissed as vagrants.

(Northumberland Record Office Access No. QSO 5)

So the male Faws were convicted as Rogues and Vagabonds but escaped justice while four of the women in this gang were whipped through Morpeth then released. But this would also involve the women being put out of the town. The records do not make it clear whether the justices kept the children of these Faws in their care at that time or whether some Faws children came back into the custody of the county later, probably the latter given the ages of the children. But there are two significant entries in the sessions records four years later that make it clear the authorities had not caught up with the escaped 'Baileys alias ffawes' and that the justices were dealing with the problem of the Faws children with compassion and humanity despite the problems caused by their parents. The older children were given the chance to learn a respectable trade through apprenticeships paid for by the authorities and the younger children were awarded a weekly

Thomas Bewick depicts a whipping in Aesop's Fables.

allowance for their maintenance.

Northumberland Quarter Sessions Order Book 1710 – 1719

Christmas Sessions, 14 January 1716/17 at Morpeth

Bailey and other Vagabonds. Whereas William Bailey and divers others stand indicted and convicted as Vagabonds and Incorrigible Rogues and do now wander & lurke in divers parts of this County and do affright and terrify his Majesties subjects. It is ordered that warrants issue out to the severall High and petty Constables of this County for taking and apprehending the said persons and them to convey to His Majesties Gaols in this County there to remain and be processed ag't according to Law and Justice.

Bailey alias ffawes Children. William Bailey aged 12 years to be bound apprentice by Indenture to Robt' Glendenning who is to have forty shillings with him as his binding money, James Bailey aged ten years to be bound out by Indenture to Thomas Maddison who is to have three pounds binding money, Marjery aged 4 years and Patrick aged three years and Henry aged three quarters of a year, children of William and Patrick Bailey to have allowed them weekly for their maintenance and clothing five shillings and six pence, and Henry son of Robert Carr one year old to have allowed two shillings weekly, Patrick eight years old son of the said Robert Carr to be bound apprentice to Matthew Lambert Brickmaker who is to have three pounds with him as his binding money. It is ordered that the Treasurer pay the severall sums to Cuthbert Marshall for this purpose. [NB payments to Cuthbert Marshall for the maintenance of the younger children are to be found in the records for several years afterwards.]

(Northumberland Record Office Access No. QSO 5)

There is no record of William Bailey and the other escapees being arrested in Northumberland.

In 1742 two boys from the Faws put their lives at risk by committing sacrilege:

This week two boys, both of them under sixteen, were committed to Morpeth Jail, for robbing the Parish Church of Ovingham in this County of the Service Plate &c.

Newcastle Courant Saturday 1 January 1742/3

These two boys were Charles and William Graham. In August 1743 they were sentenced to death at the Northumberland Assizes for the offence of sacrilege at Ovingham. However, before leaving Newcastle the Judge, Thomas Birch, Sergeant at Law, reprieved the two boys. They were held in Morpeth Gaol for more than a year then transported to America for 14 years. The costs of moving the Grahams and other prisoners to the south of England in 1745 are recorded in the Northumberland Quarter Sessions Order Books: £1 16s 0d to transport them to the Tyne then £5 each to the ship's master, Matthew Giles, to take them by sea to either the Thames or a south coast port for the journey across the Atlantic Ocean. No records now survive to establish whether the boy William Graham who survived the death sentence in 1743 was the same person as the man William Graham hanged alongside William Cockburn at Morpeth in 1788 for housebreaking.

The most well known of the 18th century Faws must be the Northumbrian piper, James Allan, a popular musician, who travelled the world one step ahead of prison and the gallows or firing squad for most of his extraordinary life and was to have several biographies written about him soon after his death. He was the sixth son of William Allan, one of the Northumberland Faws. His exact age is something of a mystery, his birth being given as 1720 or 1734 in various books with the latter being supported by a baptism entry in the Rothbury Parish Church records as 21 April 1734. Clearly Allan was born somewhere near Rothbury but the place is variously reported as Hepple, Rothbury Forest, Whitehouses and Woodhouses.

William Allan was 'a celebrated player' of the Northumbrian pipes and he

James Allen, from James Thompson's biography of 1828.

James Allen 'received into the class of minstrels', from James Thompson's biography of 1828.

taught his son James to play. The boy soon revealed a rare skill as a musician. Andrew Wight, one of his biographers, writing in 1818, said that James Allan 'At the age of sixteen frequented fairs, weddings and merry meetings, where the superior sweetness of his melody always procured him a welcome reception and a handsome reward.' His skill earned him favour with the Duke and Duchess of Northumberland and he twice held appointments as piper at Alnwick Castle. A famous engraving of James Allan shows him wearing the Saracen's Crescent of the Percy family on his right sleeve. Allan was hardly ever separated from his pipes in his lifetime and whatever scrape he got into, and there were many of them, he always ensured that the pipes escaped with him.

His gifts as a musician and his charm should have ensured a comfortable and profitable life style, but he had no wish to put down roots and was blighted by wander-lust, romantic scrapes and that inability, so typical of the Faws, to resist even petty fraud and crimes. Frequently he raised money by accepting bounty from military recruiting officers and then deserting the regiment at the first opportunity. Of course, this led to him being on the run from various military search parties. To escape he went to sea and travelled

James Allen 'terrifies the soldiers with his pipe drones and escapes', from James Thompson's biography of 1828.

throughout the world visiting Africa, India, China, Russia and many other countries. On one occasion he was sentenced to death for desertion in France, but with a comrade was given a last minute reprieve on a promise of good behaviour. Allan's response to that generous decision was to desert again within a day or two and return to England.

Desertion by James Allen and the use of his pipes came together in an extraordinary way in 1761. No 'sweetness of melody' was involved, just ingenuity and quickness of mind.

> On Wednesday James Allen, a notorious Deserter, in the Custody of a Party of the Yorkshire West-Riding Militia, made his Escape from them, by the following Stratagem, viz. He made a Pretence of to go out of the Road a little, and while only a Centinel with a drawn Sword in his Hand was along with him, he pulled out his Bag-Pipes, clapped them, to his Breast, and swore he would shoot him: The other taking it for a Pistol, turn'd about to get more Assistance, but the Piper, made the best of his Way off.

Newcastle Journal Saturday 17 January 1761

James Allen 'escapes from his guards', from James Thompson's biography of 1828.

On another occasion he flirted with the gallows by being arrested for horse-stealing at Wooler.

> Thursday James Allen, the noted piper, was apprehended in this town, on suspicion of stealing some horses lately mentioned in this paper, and yesterday was examined before Walter Trevelyan Esq.: who committed him to Morpeth Gaol.

Newcastle Courant Saturday 10 August 1776

This magistrate, Walter Trevelyan of Netherwitton, was the man who relentlessly pursued the Faws and, 14 years later, was so deeply involved in the prosecution of the Winter Gang for murder at Elsdon. Allen was confined in the County Gaol at Morpeth but when he came up for trial at the Northumberland Assizes at Newcastle at the end of July 1777 he was acquitted on a technicality. His luck finally ran out in May 1803, when he stole a horse from a stable at Gateshead and was tracked down and arrested at Lillis Leaf in Roxburghshire. The Tyneside newspapers reported the result of his trial at Durham Assizes:

> At Durham Assizes (i.e. on 3rd August) James Allan of North Shields the

famous piper aged 77, for stealing a horse out of the stable of Matthew Robinson of Gateshead, was found Guilty, Death......

Before the Judges left town they were pleased to reprieve James Allan (the piper) and Thomas Davison condemned for horse-stealing and burglary.

Newcastle Courant
Saturday 6 August 1803

James Allen in old age.

Allan's death sentence was commuted to transportation to Australia, however a decision was taken to detain Allan in Durham Gaol because of his age and ill health. Well-wishers negotiated a pardon for him but it arrived too late. He died in prison on 13 November 1810 and was buried in Elvet Churchyard in Durham.

There are many references to Faws in 18th century records, for example, Eneas Mackenzie in his *History of Northumberland* (1822) describes how in 1792 or 1793 the magistrate Walter Trevelyan of Netherwitton led a party of magistrates and constables to clear the Faws out of cottages formerly occupied by pitmen at Hepple. The officials then set fire to the houses and burned them to the ground

Traditionally the nomadic Faws gathered at Rothbury in Northumberland. John Wesley referred to this practice in his Journals: 'Monday 17th June 1782. I preached at Rothbury in the Forest, formerly a nest of Banditti; now as quiet a place as any in the County'.

Thirty years earlier there was abundant evidence of a 'nest of Banditti' in the Rothbury district and of their desperate conduct. For example, over the Christmas period in 1751 some Faws were held at Morpeth Gaol, convicted at the Northumberland Quarter Sessions on 15 January 1751/2 and sentenced to be transported.

Three weeks later there was serious trouble with the prisoners in the county gaol. According to the *Newcastle Journal* Saturday 15 February 1751/2, on the previous Friday the felons at Morpeth attempted to escape. After having their irons filed off, they came downstairs in a body and attacked the gaoler, the turnkey and the gaoler's wife and sister. They threatened to kill them unless they handed over the keys to the gaol. Fortunately neighbours heard the commotion and came to help so the escape attempt failed.

Shortly afterwards Peter Brown, a boy of around 14 or 15, was arrested and charged with passing files to the prisoners to use in their escape. According to the *Journal*:

> He is brother to one Charles Brown* who broke into Ovingham Church some years ago, and was transported in 1744. As he is one of the Rothbury Gang of Faws and doubtless has committed several Felonies, it is hoped that the Persons they have committed upon, will charge him with them whilst he is in Gaol.

> *The two boys who broke into Ovingham church in 1743 and were transported in 1744 were convicted under the names of Charles and William Graham, so either they or Peter Brown were using an alias. But that was common amongst the Faws, they used either surname of their father and mother or any other name as suited their purpose.

Within a few days the authorities arrested members of the Faw Gang from the Rothbury area for stealing goods from shops at Morpeth. This short report in the *Newcastle Gazette* probably conceals an intensive operation by the magistrates and parish constables to capture the troublesome Faws.

We have advice from Rothbury that yesterday sennight seven of the Faws who have so long infested that Town and neighbourhood were apprehended and are since committed to Morpeth Gaol. Several more were pursued to the mountains but could not be come at because of the snow &c. We are also informed that some of the goods lately stolen out of the shops at Morpeth were found in their custody.

Newcastle Gazette 19 February 1751/2

The authorities were, no doubt, pleased to reassure the public by announcing 13 more arrests in March. The next sitting of the Northumberland Quarter Sessions was held at Morpeth on 8 April 1752. George Cant, the county gaoler at that time, and his family would be much relieved, given the violence of the attempted escape from prison, at not having to transport this dangerous gang to some other part of the county for trial. Peter Brown, who had assisted in the attempted escape from gaol (helped by two Faws women who provided the files to remove fetters from the prisoners), was ordered to be transported to the plantations in America for seven years. Brown was accompanied there by all the other Faws prisoners convicted of various crimes and being 'Rogues, Vagabonds and Sturdy Beggars.'

It was at these sessions that the Justices decided to make the standing offer of rewards for the arrest and conviction of the Faws quoted at the opening of this chapter. The Quarter Sessions records show that several rewards were actually paid out following the convictions described here.

The Justices wasted no time in beginning the transportation process. On Monday 13 April 1752, five days after sentence, the Faws were put on board a ship named the *Owner's Goodwill* commanded by Captain Martin Moorland. The master had agreed with the county authorities to carry the prisoners south for transportation for a fee of £5 each. The Faws were joined by other prisoners from the Newgate Gaol at Newcastle. Such journeys were not without danger. On its last voyage the *Owner's Goodwill*, under a different master, had run aground near Wells in Norfolk. Fortunately on that occasion no lives were lost and the greater part of the cargo had been saved.

Just over two years later, in July 1754, the public were advised that 15 members of this gang 'commonly called or known by the name Faws' had returned unlawfully from transportation and rewards were offered for their capture. The notice published in the *Newcastle Journal* on 27 July 1754 is interesting for the graphic descriptions including the fact that the faces of many of this gang of Faws were 'marked with the Small Pox.' For example 'William Fall is about 27 years of age, 5 Feet 10 Inches high, and of a swarthy complexion; and Jane otherwise Ann, his Wife, is a strong short made Woman, and marked with the Small Pox.'

There is a tale about the Faws that reveals a great deal about their life style. It is an account of the life and death of Richard Clarke, born near Berwick-upon-Tweed about 1739 and died on the gallows at York in 1767. His parents, Robert and Elizabeth Clarke, were among the Faws transported from Morpeth Gaol in April 1752.

The *Newcastle Journal* for Saturday 25 April 1767 reported the execution in York of Richard Clarke for breaking into the house of Mark Hattersley near Knaresborough, and stealing 24 guineas and some clothes. Clarke left an account of his life in his own handwriting. He was born at Spital, near Berwick-upon-Tweed in 1739. About a year after his parents were transported he met a cousin at Richmond fair, who had returned from transportation. Before long he was reunited with his father and mother, who had also returned from transportation. They travelled about the country as pedlars and Clarke sometimes went to school. The family travelled to Ireland, where they were imprisoned for theft, but discharged for lack of evidence. They returned to England, where they continued housebreaking, horse stealing and pocket picking. The story continues:

> About eight years ago he was convicted at the assizes here of a highway robbery and transported, but returned again in less than a year and joined his father and mother with the rest of the gang. In 1762, he was convicted of horse-stealing at Shrewsbury, where he received sentence of death, but was reprieved the day before that fixed for his execution, and afterwards transported to Maryland, from whence he also soon returned, and coming to Warrington in Lancashire, he was informed of his wife being hanged at Coventry.

> He then went in quest of his mother and met with her at Newcastle. A short time after he was committed to Carlisle Gaol for house-breaking, of which he was convicted and, in 1765, transported to Virginia, but soon returned from thence and met with his mother once more at Newcastle, and broke into several houses last summer, but got little money or other effects, except from a house near Durham, from whence he took about £13, and what he got in Mark Hattersley's house, for which he suffered.

> Several times, when short of money he enlisted for a soldier, but always soon deserted.

This report appears to be a reliable account of Clarke's life as many parts of it can be verified in various archives. Clarke's wife was executed at

Coventry on Wednesday 10 August 1763 after being found guilty of unlawfully returning from a sentence of transportation. Richard Clarke was convicted at the Cumberland Assizes at Carlisle in the summer of 1765, transported again, but returned unlawfully only to pick up his old criminal activities ending on the gallows at York in 1767; quite a remarkable career surviving at least one actual death sentence and the risk of three others for returning from transportation.

It is clear then that the Faws were dangerous, determined, persistent criminals active throughout the 18th century in the North East, the borders and elsewhere. Many of them returned early from transportation. The death penalty for returning illegally appears to have been perceived as a risk worth taking. No sex or age group was safe from them as is clearly illustrated in this final example, the story of James McFidum alias Macfarlane executed at Durham on Monday 27 August 1750.

An eight year-old boy was on his way from his home at Gibside to school. Passing through Whickham Common he saw a man sitting with a woman on his knee. The man struck up a conversation with the boy, then dragged him into a hollow, removed all his clothes except his coat and breeches and threatened to cut his throat from ear to ear if he cried out. As soon as the boy was set free he went to find his father who alerted the neighbours and set off in pursuit of the villain. The man was soon caught and sent to Durham gaol.

> The Fellow pretended to be dumb when before the Justice; but the Boy put him in mind of the Speech he made when he threaten'd his Life. This Man and the above mentioned Woman, are said to belong to a Gang, well known by the Name Faws, who for many Years have much infested the Northern Counties.
>
> *Newcastle Journal* Saturday 1 September 1750

The same day (i.e. last Monday 27 August) James McFidum alias Macfarlane was executed at Durham for robbing Robert Hopes, a boy about ten years old. He died penitent, but denied his being guilty of the Fact for which he suffered. (*Newcastle Journal* Saturday 13 January 1749/50)

This should have been a salutary warning to criminals in the North East, however within two years it happened again, this time at Hexham, and the villain escaped.

There are hints here and there of the existence of a leader of the Faws. He is a shadowy figure at best, with little known about him or what power or control, if any, he may have had over the gangs. The Tyneside newspapers in June 1752 carried reports of the detention of the so-called King of the Faws. The accounts are tantalising in the lack of detail:

No more reports about this man appeared in the local newspapers.

Last Sunday a well dressed man was apprehended and carried to the Tower on the Bridge on suspicion being the Principal of a Sett of People called the Faws; and on Monday he was had before the Right Worshipful the Mayor, but not being able to give a Satisfactory account of himself, was committed to Newgate.
Newcastle Gazette Wednesday 3 June 1752

This week a man pretty well dressed was apprehended on suspicion of being one of the Rothbury Faws; and as he could not give a satisfactory account of himself, when examined before a Magistrate, he was committed to Newgate. Some accounts received since confirm the above and also add that this very man is the King of the aforesaid Gang of Faws, or Sturdy Beggars.
Newcastle Journal Saturday 6 June 1752

Records for offenders appearing at the Mayor's Court at Newcastle upon Tyne at that time have not survived. What little information there is ends nearly four years later with this entry in the 18th century burial register of the parish church of Jarrow:

Buried – 13th January 1756. Francis Heron, King of ye Faws.

6. Gaols of Northumberland

> On Monday (June 15th 1789) the prisoners in Morpeth gaol attempted to make their escape. They had got their irons sawed off, broke open the inner door of the prison, knocked down the turnkey, and on the gaoler's entering, finding they could not escape, they took him prisoner, and made fast the door of their apartment.
> Fortunately, a party of artillery were then in the town, and by their assistance, they were quelled and properly secured.
>
> (*Newcastle Chronicle* Saturday 20 June 1789)

Strictly speaking, the principal gaols for each shire county and county borough in the United Kingdom were the 'King's Gaols', but in fact the financial and management responsibility lay with the justices acting for the High Sheriff. Each county was required to have two gaols: one for debtors and the other, the county gaol, for felons. The debtors' gaol and county gaol, in one building, for Northumberland was at Morpeth. For the greater part of the 18th century the gaoler was not paid a salary but relied for his income on fees paid by the prisoners. The maintenance of the gaol and running costs were paid from county funds as approved by the justices at Quarter Sessions. The prisoners held in the county gaol included prisoners for Quarter Sessions as well as the Northumberland Assizes, unlike Newcastle upon Tyne, for example, where other arrangements were made for Quarter Sessions prisoners. The gaoler was forbidden by law to mix the debtors and felons.

According to John Hodgson (*History of Morpeth* 1832), some part of the castle at Morpeth was in use as the county gaol at the time of Cardinal Wolsey (1471-1530). By 1603 a tower in what is now Bridge Street, Morpeth, was the county gaol. The building was rented from the Earl of Carlisle by the High Sheriff, appointed each year, who, it would appear, paid the rent from his own resources. That arrangement continued until the beginning of the 18th century when an interesting story begins with a former High Sheriff, William Wilkinson, complaining about the expense of the gaol rent falling on successive High Sheriffs, when the county should have paid it.

However John Impey, in his book *The Office of Sheriff*, 1786, makes it clear the High Sheriff was responsible for the gaols as the King's representative and the justices may have been thinking that the High Sheriff should follow tradition in Northumberland. However, the justices were soon to find the county was facing much greater expense and long-term financial commitment on the gaols.

At the Northumberland Assizes in August 1702, the judges imposed a fine of £2,000 on the county for 'not haveing a sufficient gaol.' This was a means of applying pressure on county authorities to provide adequate and secure premises for prisoners. The county justices met in an adjourned sessions at Newcastle upon Tyne the day after the Assizes ended.
They appointed three of their number to view the gaoler's house, gardens and other buildings adjoining the gaol at Morpeth and consider whether they would be suitable for the county to buy for the building of a gaol, and how much the property was worth. They were to report their findings to Mr Lisle, the Clerk of the Peace, who would correspond with the Earl of Carlisle.

The justices met at the Michaelmass Sessions at Alnwick on 7 October 1702 and there was considerable lobbying to create a new county gaol there. Alnwick offered the Tower Gate at Clayport, next door to the House of Correction, to use as a gaol at a rent of 12 pence a year. An alternative would be to convert the House of Correction (reported to be very much in decay, with much of the timber missing) into a gaol.

Was all of this lobbying motivated by a desire on the part of some gentlemen of the county to bring about change and make Alnwick the power-base of county affairs? If that were the motive it came to nothing as a decision to build at Morpeth was made at the next Christmas Sessions held at Morpeth on 13th January 1702/03, 'this court being unanimously of the opinion that Morpeth is a more convenient place for building and making a sufficient Gaoll for the service of the County ...'. (Northumberland Record Office Access No. QSO 4)

The new gaol at Morpeth was built on the site of the old one. The justices raised funds by ordering an assessment of 20 shillings in the pound 'on all lands etc.,' in the county. The decision to build the gaol at Bridge Street, Morpeth was taken at the Easter Sessions at Morpeth on 7 April 1703. The justices made funds available to the county surveyor, George Barker, and also a man named James Quincey 'to view the gaoll and make a draught (plan) for the making and modifying the Gaoll etc.' Quincey appears to have been a designer-cum-builder. John Hodgson recorded the cost of the new prison as £1,337 15s 10½d, and that it was finished by 30 November 1704. The Bridge Street prison served Northumberland as the debtors' prison and county gaol until 15 December 1828. This prison building was inspected by John Howard, the famous prison reformer, five times between 1774 and 1782.

The new gaol at Morpeth, photographed in 1993.

Barry Redfern

The highest number of criminal prisoners seen by John Howard in Morpeth Gaol at one time was 11 in January 1776. There were 15 debtors in March 1782. According to Howard, the building had six 'sizeable' rooms for debtors and a court (an open space) for them to exercise in. He said that the felons were always shut up in the 'tower', which contained one room for women and two for men. The first was a day room measuring 14ft 2ins by 6ft 9ins, and the other 'an offensive dungeon' measuring 18ft by 9ft with one window. Stone walls, 10 or 12ft high, enclosed the grounds between the gaol and the river and the remains of the walls can be seen there today. In 1776 Howard found three transports (prisoners sentenced to be transported to the colonies in America or the West Indies) chained to a ring in the floor on suspicion of planning to escape. There were many occasions throughout the 18th century when the numbers of prisoners was much greater than Howard found on his visits and the congestion in the cells caused great problems for the gaolers.

By 1818 significant changes had taken place at Morpeth Gaol. A survey published in Parliamentary Papers revealed that there were now ten cells for debtors capable of holding 44 prisoners, plus a debtors' day room also used as a chapel. For the felons there were now three cells used as solitary cells with one prisoner in each, plus a room used as a sleeping cell that had contained eight prisoners. Those male felons also had the use of a day room. The room for female felons had contained eight prisoners. One hundred prisoners had been committed to Morpeth Gaol in 1818 (British Parliamentary Papers, Crime and Punishment, Prisons 1818-1822 (135) Vol. XVII).

On 26 August 1818, Joseph John Gurney and his sister Elizabeth Fry visited Morpeth Gaol. They published reports on their prison visits in much the same way as John Howard. They found the prison to be old and defective but neat and tidy. They complimented the gaoler and his wife, John and Elizabeth Blake: 'The prisoners are ruled by the law of kindness; chains are therefore unnecessary for them. They appeared to us to be subdued and softened by the gentleness with which they were treated.'

This report reveals that in 1818 the allowance paid by the county for maintaining the prisoners, that is to say for feeding them, was fourpence per day. At the time of John Howard's visits in the 18th century it was twopence per day. John Howard firmly believed that gaolers should live on the premises or close by; he saw too many examples throughout the country of gaolers leaving the running of the gaol to their staff, rarely visiting the prison and even then never entering the cells. The Morpeth gaoler had quarters for his family inside the prison.

The gaolers were appointed by the justices at the Quarter Sessions but were acting on behalf of the High Sheriff of Northumberland as John Impey made clear in *The Office of Sheriff*, 1786 'Gaolers are also the servants of the sheriff and he must be responsible for their actions.' Impey had a poor opinion of gaolers and pointed out that the law required gaolers to treat prisoners with humanity and not subject them to hardships other than those that were absolutely necessary for their confinement. Unfortunately the measures that were absolutely necessary were left to the gaolers, who, because they were so used to scenes of misery, were frequently merciless and lacking in humanity, to define.

This is an incomplete list of the gaolers at the gaol at Bridge Street, Morpeth.

> 1696, Ralph READ
> c1711 – c1724, Edward GREY
> 1742 – 1744, William LOWES
> (Turnkey – George CANT)
> 1746 – 1748, Thomas USHER
> 1748 – 1760, George CANT
> 1760 – 1772, Dorothy CANT
> 1772 – 1787, John KENT
> 1787 – 1838, John BLAKE

Living within the prison was not without danger for the gaoler and his family. The suffering of George Cant, his wife Dorothy and the turnkey in a mass escape attempt from Morpeth Gaol is described in the chapter on the Faws. Only the intervention and support of neighbours saved them from severe injury or death. Dorothy Cant must have been a strong character; she became the gaoler herself following the death of her husband in 1761. Mrs Cant held the post for more than ten years. Not a lot is known about the gaolers. George Cant had been the turnkey to one of his predecessors William Lowes. The turnkey was the gaoler's right-hand man, something akin to a deputy, and had the right to discharge fees from prisoners. John

Kent was gaoler during John Howard's visits to Morpeth Gaol but Howard made no direct comment about him.

More is known about John Blake: he was appointed gaoler in April 1787 and three weeks later married Elizabeth Hogg at St John's Parish Church, Newcastle. This newly-wed couple lived on an income derived from a system of charges and fees to criminal and debtor prisoners, and a licence to sell liquors to the prisoners all authorised by the justices at Quarter Sessions. John Howard recorded the fees at Morpeth Gaol: 'On commitment to gaol each felon was required to pay 2s 8d to the gaoler, and on discharge 18s 4d to the gaoler and 2s 0d to the turnkey, a total of £1 3s 0d'. The fees were payable whether the prisoner was convicted or not. If the prisoner could not pay he remained in gaol. It was the injustice of requiring prisoners cleared by courts to pay fees that set John Howard off on his life's work. Howard made some progress towards getting rid of gaoler's fees in his lifetime but the Gaol Fees Abolition Act of 1815 finally prohibited the practice.

Towards the end of the 18th century, the Northumberland Justices had begun to pay the fees of acquitted prisoners, then introduced a part-salary part-fees policy for the gaoler, but it was not until 1824 that Northumberland actually abolished the payment of fees by prisoners and substituted fixed salaries for officials in the county institutions. Money was needed for other prison costs, of course, and sometimes the claims to the treasurer were for a very mixed bag of expenses, revealing much about day-to-day prison life.

At the Northumberland Quarter Sessions, 25 April 1811, £101 17s 9½d was ordered to be paid to John Blake, Gaoler at Morpeth. The money was to reimburse him for a wide range of expenses including clothes for two female prisoners and the cost of

> conveying them for Transportation; an inquest upon a deceased prisoner and expenses for his funeral; shaving poor prisoners; the Turnkey's wages for the previous quarter; straw; coals; sweeping chimneys; wine for the use of the chapel; and fees for attending the prisoners' church service for the previous year.
>
> (Northumberland Record Office Access No. QSO17)

John Blake appears to have been a sympathetic and supportive gaoler,

Morpeth market place in the late 18th century.

Gurney and Fry reported favourably; he put prisoners in irons only when there was thought be a danger of escape and he was credited with stopping the practice of allowing the public to pay to view prisoners in the dungeon of the Keep on Assize Sunday. The justices complimented him in 1811 and his salary increased.

When the Bridge Street gaol closed in December 1828, John Blake was appointed the first governor or keeper of the new county gaol, designed by the Newcastle architect John Dobson, which stood on the south side of the River Wansbeck where the police station is today. The Prisons Act of 1835 (5 & 6 WILLIAM IV c.38), amongst other things, established the first government inspectors of prisons. In the same year Frederic Hill, a 32-year-old barrister and parliamentary secretary, was appointed as the inspector of prisons for Scotland, Northumberland and Durham. It was not until 1838 that he was able to report on the principal prisons in Northumberland and Durham. Hill's opinions on prison affairs caused quite stir in the north east and in particular an idea that prisoners in confinement for long periods should be transferred to Carlisle Prison. His recommendations in that respect were not taken up. However so far as the future for John Blake as the keeper of Morpeth Gaol was concerned the report was quite devastating.

> OFFICERS ... The keeper appears to be intelligent, kind hearted and trustworthy, but it is sufficient to state he is now 80 years old, to show that he must be unable energetically to discharge the duties of his office.

(3rd Report of the Inspectors Appointed to Visit the Different Prisons of Great Britain, 1838)

The Justices at the Quarter Sessions appointed James Cousins, Keeper of the House of Correction at Alnwick, to be the new Keeper of the County Gaol and sent him to London for two months to study best practice at Brixton and other prisons of the Metropolis. John Blake remained to oversee the gaol.

John Blake retired in the summer of 1838 with a generous pension, having spent 51 years in charge of the gaol. His salary when he retired was £210. John Blake told Frederic Hill he had never been attacked or even insulted in 50 years as a gaoler. But that claim is difficult to reconcile with the quotation at the opening of this chapter and the following report two years after his appointment at the Northumberland County Gaol.

> The riotous behaviour of the felons in Morpeth Gaol, where a great number are confined, has arisen to such height that the gaoler is under the necessity of calling in the assistance of the military. The cause of such riots seems to be owing to the want of separate cells to keep them apart, or to the increase of the number of convicts destined for Botany Bay, who not being quickly sent off, through long confinement, generally become desperate.
>
> *Newcastle Courant* Saturday 20 June 1789

At the Northumberland Quarter Sessions at Hexham in July 1789 there were 15 prisoners put up for trial. In August there were 20 prisoners put up for trial at the Northumberland Assizes. At the Northumberland Assizes the previous year four prisoners were sentenced to be transported, so if there were transports that had not been moved on still at Morpeth Gaol then there must have been great pressure on space in June of 1789 and enormous potential for trouble.

Prisoners hatching plans to escape were a constant hazard for the county gaolers and their staff and overcrowding in prison inevitably led to problems. To put irons on prisoners was one widely used practice to deter escape, but prisoners seem to have been ingenious in finding ways to remove them. Close contact with each other made planning an escape easy. It is hardly surprising that there were many escape attempts in the 18th century. The authorities would take action if they thought there were shortcomings on the part of the gaol staff. The county gaoler, Edward Grey, was fined £5 in 1724 'for suffering Thomas Rawson to be at large.'

The poor state of health of prisoners and close association meant that infectious diseases could pass rapidly through a gaol. Morpeth Gaol had a 'surgeon' appointed by the justices at the Quarter Sessions. In the 18th century the surgeons for Morpeth Gaol were:

> 17?? – 1747, John Chandler (died in post)
> 1747 – 1792, Francis Laidman
> 1792 – 1800, John Laidman (died in post)
> 1800 – 1810, Douglas Sands
> 1811 – 1837, William Hawdon (died in post)
> Appointed 1837, Robert Hawdon

'Appointment' of these surgeons should not be seen as an arrangement for full-time medical staff constantly tending prisoners and monitoring their health. They were simply country or town doctors called in by the gaoler when necessary. The doctors were not paid a salary but received fees for their services. What medical problems faced the gaol surgeons at Morpeth in the 18th century are now lost in time. There were not less than 39 deaths in Morpeth Gaol from 1679 through to 1788 that can be traced through the Morpeth Parish Church records. No records of the causes of these deaths have survived.

There were also two baptisms from the gaol and at least one marriage – 2 January 1778, Thomas son of Thomas and Ann THOMPSON and 3 May 1778 Joseph, son of Joseph WINHAM and Mary BROWN 'in ye gaol.'

The following curious extract is from the Morpeth Register 28th September 1711 John Brown and Esther Borne after three times calling was married in

the Gaol, by reason he could not get liberty to come to church, and Susanna their daughter was baptised the same day and the bride was churched that day also.

Berwick-upon-Tweed Advertiser Saturday 27 January 1849

There is a simple entry for 1 March 1751 recording the death of Thomas Armstrong alias William Cooper alias 'Socky Tom' who, with William Booth was arrested in 1750 for horse stealing. They were both convicted and sentenced to death at the Northumberland Assizes in August. However the judges reprieved both men from the death sentence. The *Newcastle Journal* newspaper report revealed a startling fact about 'Socky Tom.'

Newcastle August 18th

At the conclusion of the Assizes for this Town and County ... Thomas Armstrong alias Cooper alias Socky Tom, and William Booth, both condemned for Horse-stealing, were reprieved by the Judges before they left Town. Socky Tom, said to be 92 years old, is ordered to be imprisoned for life, Booth ...to lie in Gaol until the next Assizes then to be Transported for Life.

Newcastle Journal Saturday 25 August, 1750

Ninety-two years of age must be some sort of a record for a death sentence whether reprieved or not. Life imprisonment for Armstrong in the county gaol was a very unusual step by the judges, but their assessment of the likely future for Armstrong was correct. He lived only about six months longer and it is unlikely he would have survived crossing the Atlantic Ocean in a convict ship.

Frederic Hill's report of 1838, on the new gaol, provides the earliest surviving detail about prisoners' health problems, 'The ordinary complaints are constipation of the bowels, itch and venereal diseases; the bowel complaints being generally brought on, the surgeon thinks, by want of exercise.' (3rd Report of the Inspectors Appointed to Visit the Different Prisons of Great Britain, 1838)

The physical well-being of prisoners rested with the surgeons, but spiritual welfare was a matter for the chaplains. The earliest records show that the justices paid a salary to a clergymen to act as chaplain to the gaol.

The salary was £5 per year in the 17th century, then £10 from early in 18th century until 1773, then over the next 50 years or so the salary rose steadily, 1775 – £20, 1776 – £30, 1813 – £40 and 1827 – £50. The chaplains were faced with the day-to-day challenge of counselling, prayers and divine service for men, women and, occasionally, child prisoners. Some were hardened and impervious to the teaching of the church, with little to look forward to in life, others were less so. But all were in need of someone to set standards and guide them to a better way of life. It must have been a daunting task for the chaplains. They were often the curates of local churches and the pastoral care of prisoners was a part-time task for them. Not all the clergymen were up to the task; in 1697 the prisoners at Morpeth Gaol petitioned the justices for the removal of the Rev. Stephen Jackson 'who is a person of very negligent, loose and roundabout life.' There must have been some justification for the petition as the chaplain was replaced at once. But the deep concern of the clergy that shines through all the surviving records was that condemned prisoners should repent. Some of the chaplains, usually styled 'The Rev. Mr', remained in post for quite long periods.

c1681 – 1691, Rev. Mr John Pye

1691 – 1697, Rev. Mr Stephen Jackson

1697 – 1698, Rev. Mr Isaac Wallis (or Wallas) (Died in post)

1698 – , Rev. Mr Gabriel Martin

1714 – 1716, Rev. Mr George Fenwick with Rev. Thomas Richardson

1717 – 1718, Rev. Mr George Fenwick

1719 – 1722, Rev. Mr George Fenwick and Rev. Mr. George Gordon

1722 – 1759, Rev. Mr George Gordon (Died in post)

1759 – 1763, Rev. Mr Coxon

1763 – 1773, Rev. Mr Holden

1773 – 1827, Rev. Mr Edward Nicholson (Died in post)

1828 – 1834, Rev. Mr Luke Yarker

1835 – , Rev. Mr Thomas Shute (In post 1838)

The confinement and control of debtor prisoners caused fewer problems for the county gaolers than the unruly and undisciplined prisoners on the criminal side. Guarding against escape was important because the gaoler may then have to assume responsibility for the debts of the escapee. But generally speaking, no irons were needed for them and the debtors had much more freedom. At the Bridge Street Gaol there was an open-air yard at the back of the building for them to walk in and arrangements could be made for them to carry on their trade if possible. Just how that worked in practice is lost in time now; presumably there could be problems with tools of the trade being in a gaol and how did such tradesmen communicate and deal with their clients? Somehow they needed to raise money, not only to pay off their debts but also to pay the gaoler's fees, 12s 6d on commitment and 10s 2d on discharge. There was no allowance paid to them for food (the county fed the criminal prisoners) but destitute debtor prisoners could apply to the justices at the sessions for an allowance. Generous donations were made by county gentlemen from time to time to help debtor prisoners. The Duke of Northumberland, for example, sent £200 to the High Sheriff of Northumberland 'to be by him disposed of towards the release of poor persons confined in Morpeth Gaol for small debts'.

According to John Howard, debtor prisoners without resources were held in 'a large room that the prisoners pay nothing for, which holds a great many beds, called Middle Tower.' There were also rooms available for rent by debtors; these were quaintly known as 'Burton's Room, Mrs Carr's Room, the Green Room, Mr Johnson's Room and were available with bedding provided by the gaoler at three shillings and six-pence per week or slightly less for two prisoners sharing.' Perhaps the rooms acquired their names from long-term residents for debt. Morpeth Gaol had its share of those:

> Died – Saturday the 7th inst. in Morpeth jail, after a confinement of seven years and one month, Mr Lionel Forster late of Corsenside.
>
> *Newcastle Chronicle or Weekly Advertiser*, Saturday 14 June 1788

Deaths of debtors in prison were commonplace and if they died without funds a gaoler, in some parts of the country, might go to extraordinary lengths to recover his discharge fees:

> Humanity of a Gaoler. Monday (15th June 1789) died in the King's Bench Prison, Mr Omer, an attorney. This unfortunate man, being found guilty of poverty, inasmuch as not to be able to liquidate honest Lockit's demand for fees, his carcase was arrested by the Marshal, and actually sold to Mr Longbottom, an anatomist, for three guineas, to defray the same.
>
> *Newcastle Chronicle* Saturday 20 June 1789

The county gaol at Bridge Street, Morpeth was closed on 15 December 1828. The prison buildings are still there today. The remains of the prison yard wall can be seen at the back of the premises. The new county gaol, designed by John Dobson lasted until 20 October 1881, when it was closed and the prisoners transferred to Newcastle. Management of prisons passed from the local authorities to the new Prison Commissioners in 1877. One of their first tasks was to review the spread of prisons about the country and as a consequence of that review many prisons were closed. The site of John Dobson's prison was redeveloped as a police station for the county police, but the substantial gatehouse was used for many years as a courthouse.

All of the 18th century Northumberland Assizes were held in the old Moot Hall at Castlegarth, on county land in the middle of Newcastle, next to the Keep. There were no cells in the old Moot Hall and for the short period of the court sitting, usually about a week, the prisoners were held in the dungeon of the Keep in wretched and often wet conditions. The dungeon was open to the air at that time. The justices rotated the sittings of the

Northumberland Quarter Sessions around the Moot Hall at Newcastle upon Tyne, Morpeth, Hexham and Alnwick. For another short period of the year the dungeon of the Keep was in use for prisoners for the sessions. So here is one of the special problems for the county gaoler; moving prisoners in a secure way around the county towns and the need for suitable buildings to hold the prisoners. Contemporary sources show that the prisoners were heavily ironed and moved in carts on these journeys.

The need for a gaol at Hexham for Quarter Sessions prisoners and a general lock-up were met by the ancient Manor Gaol. The building can still be seen just off the Market Place near the Moot Hall. It is said to be the first purpose-built prison in England. According to the *County History of Northumberland* (Vol. III, 1896, Ed. by Alan Hinds M.A.) 'Archbishop Melton at York on 8th June 1330 ordered Thomas Fox, the receiver of Hexham, to cause a gaol to be built.' The costs were to be met by the shire of Hexham. In another order dated 19th January 1332, John de Cawode was appointed the first gaoler at Hexham at a salary of two pence per day. The gaol included a residence for the gaoler. It is apparent from

Hexham Gaol, late 19th century.

Northumberland Quarter Sessions records that in 1761 Hexham Gaol was known as the 'Manor Gaol' and William Ellis was the Keeper. The building was in use as a gaol until 1824 and is now an excellent border history museum.

There were village lock-ups dotted around the county to confine drunks and other public nuisances; examples survive at Stamfordham and Warkworth. Also linked to this problem was the requirement for the county to have a house of correction. There were several of these establishments in Northumberland between the 17th and 19th centuries. The development of such institutions goes back to the 16th century and they were part of an initiative to deal with the problem of beggars, rogues and vagabonds. In 1547 the authorities in London began an attempt to deal with such people by putting them to work in confinement in a building called Bridewell, with the objective of instilling the work ethic into them. The name originates in the old name for the building the 'Palace of St Bride's Well.' In 1576 this approach to the problem was incorporated into an Elizabethan Act of

Parliament 'for setting of the poor on work, and for avoiding idleness.' In the act the name 'House of Correction' was used for these institutions and the terms 'Bridewell' and 'House of Correction' became interchangeable. The term 'Bridewell' was not used in official Northumberland records.

Stamfordham village lock-up.

By the 18th century, however, the terms of reference and practice had widened to include short sentences of anything from 14 days to six months in the house of correction for many petty offences dealt with by the justices at sessions. A sentence to the house of correction for vagabonds and the like would quite often be combined with a whipping through the streets or public exhibition in the pillory, sometimes followed by banishment to the parish of their birth or settlement. All of this was coupled with hard work for long hours: the Morpeth House of Correction for example was for a period controlled by a clothier who put the prisoners to work in connection with his business.

In the 17th century, the house of correction for Northumberland was at Alnwick. The person in charge was known as the 'Keeper' or 'Master of the House of Correction' and was paid a salary by the county. In 1686 and through to the end of the century, John Courtney was the 'Master.' Little information has survived about the institution that stood next to the Clayport Tower in Clayport Street, a short distance from Alnwick Market Place. At the Easter Sessions in April 1686 at Morpeth the house of correction was 'presented', that is to say reported to the justices as being 'useless to the county and that it should be removed elsewhere'. In January 1703/4 the building was sold to a man called William Taylor for £110.

More than a century was to pass before Alnwick had another establishment of that kind in the town.

Representations were made for the new house of correction to be built at Hexham. It was described as the largest and most populous town in the county, situated on good corn soil.

However, after inviting other proposals, a decision was taken at the Easter Sessions at Morpeth on 15 April 1713 to build a new house of correction at Morpeth. The county authorities bought 'a house and yard and an old kiln near ye bridge end at Morpeth,' for £130. The land and buildings were on the south side of the River Wansbeck and close to the old bridge that existed in the 18th century. There were complaints about a delay in finishing the building, but the house of correction was finally opened in the autumn of 1715. It was to be a 'woollen manufactory,' organised by Thomas Ward and others. They were allowed a loan of £200 by the county authorities to set up the manufactory. The first Master of the House of Correction was Benjamin Fripp, at a salary of £30 per annum, who was followed by Benjamin Burnett then William Burnett covering most of the 18th century.

COUNTY BRIDEWELL AT MORPETH

A workroom and two small bedrooms for men on the ground floor, only seven feet high. That above the women is larger. The court not being secure, the prisoners are always locked up, and appear dirty and sickly. Over the way is a long room (72 feet) which is a warehouse and work-shop: and above it is another workshop. The keeper a clothier now lives at a distance: he employs his prisoners; the men and boys from eight o'clock to four, at two shillings per week: women from eight to five, at one shilling and six-pence a week.

(*State of the Prisons in England and Wales*, John Howard, 4th Ed 1792)

Howard found few prisoners at his visits, two in 1775, eight in 1776, three in 1779 and six in 1782. A house of correction on that site at Morpeth remained in use until the new County Gaol and House of Correction designed by John Dobson was opened nearby in December 1828. Nothing remains of the old buildings today. The site was cleared in 1830 in preparation for the new Telford Bridge and is covered by the road leading to the bridge.

In October 1744 a need was identified for a house of correction at

Hexham and the justices at the Michaelmas Sessions formally agreed to 'fix' an institution there. But, for some reason not explained in the records, the matter did not proceed. About 40 years later Hexham was at last provided with a house of correction. In 1782 parliament passed the House of Correction Act (22 Geo III c64). These new laws brought pressure to bear on county magistrates to bring about change and improvements to their houses of correction. The justices of Northumberland responded well in 1783 deciding to lease a building in Tyne Green, Hexham and convert it into a house of correction.

The Hexham House of Correction (below) was opened the same year and Joseph Daglish (sometimes referred to as Dagleas) was appointed the first Governor or Keeper at a salary of £20 per annum. It is not clear what productive work was required of the prisoners there. The building was on the left hand side of the road in the direction of Tyne Green, about 650 yards from the market place and opposite a tannery. The house of correction and the tannery buildings are still in Tyne Green Road at the corner of Cherry Lane near the bus garage. Historian A.B. Wright could find little of consequence to say about the institution in 1823.

Barry Redfern

The House of Correction is situated on Tyne Green Road. It has no claim to particular notice. In its situation or its management, there is little to blame, and this is almost the highest praise that can be bestowed upon it.

(*History of Hexham*, A.B. Wright 1823, page 109)

A new wing was added to the building in about 1827, by which time the keeper was John Leath. In February 1829 the keeper was Mr Kell and this undistinguished house of correction briefly held a notorious prisoner, Jonathan Martin, who had been arrested for setting fire to York Cathedral. He was the brother of the famous artist John Martin. The institution was still in use in 1838, when the keeper lived on the premises, but was later closed as the houses of correction were phased out.

Another response to the House of Correction Act was to build an establishment at Tynemouth; it was opened just nine years after the Hexham institution. The preliminary moves in May 1791 led to an early example of county authorities using newspapers to attract bids for public contracts:

County of Northumberland

HOUSE OF CORRECTION AT TYNEMOUTH.

Any person or persons willing to undertake the building of a House of Correction, at or near Tynemouth, in this county, according to a plan and detail thereof prepared by Mr Wm Newton, Architect, which plan and detail are deposited in the office of the Clerk of the Peace of the said county, for inspection, are desired to give in Proposals at an adjournment of the General Quarter Sessions of the Peace, to be holden at the Moothall, in Castle Garth, in the said county, on Saturday the eleventh day of June, 1791.

By Order, John Davidson, Clerk of the Peace.

Newcastle Courant Saturday 28 May 1791

Robert Robson, an innkeeper from Newcastle, was appointed as the first 'Governor or Keeper' of the Tynemouth House of Correction in April 1792. He had to provide security for the discharge of his duties and he was to be paid a salary of £20. No details have survived about the productive work Robson was to supervise in this new establishment.

A Parliamentary survey for 1818 recorded that in the building there were 14 cells of 7 feet by 6 feet six inches, plus two yards one each for male and female prisoners. By the time of Frederic Hill's first inspection of the house of correction at Tynemouth (February 1838), the building was also used to house untried prisoners. Hill found the discipline severe. It was a clean but cold prison (his visit took place in February 1838), 'there was no provision for warming the cells. The employment is of the dullest kind (picking oakum only, and that with a feeling of the work being unproductive); and even this employment is not allowed to prisoners before trial. There is, too, no provision for instruction, and none for lighting the cells in the evenings and mornings; so that in winter there are long periods of darkness and necessary idleness.' Picking oakum was the name given to a form of hard labour that was harsh on the fingers. The prisoners were supplied with pieces of old

Barry Redfern

Tynemouth House of Correction.

tarred rope from sailing ships and were required to unwind the rope and tease out the original fibre to create a stuffing material used to make ships' fenders. Each prisoner had a straw mattress, two clean blankets and three rugs.

Hill's comments on the feeding of prisoners are particularly interesting.

> **Food. The prisoners are fed entirely on bread and milk. The daily allowance to each is 3 penny rolls (together weighing about 1½ pounds at present), and a pennyworth of milk (now 2 pints). The bread, as may be expected from the price is made of fine flour. The total cost of the food is 4 pence per day each. Additional supplies from without are not permitted. I found, however, a large piece of bread that had been conveyed to one of the prisoners in his linen which his friends had had home to wash.**

> (3rd Report of the Inspectors Appointed to Visit the Different Prisons of Great Britain, 1838)

Substantial parts of the house of correction building of 1792 still stand in Tynemouth Road, opposite Tanners Bank. That section of Tynemouth Road is called Correction House Bank. Next to it is the Tynemouth Lodge Hotel that bears a blue circle commemoration plaque put up by North Tyneside Council.

NORTH TYNESIDE COUNCIL

TYNEMOUTH LODGE HOTEL
The building has been in use as a public house and residential hotel since 1799. Meals for prisoners were prepared in the cellar kitchens of this hotel and carried through an underground tunnel to the inmates of the Tynemouth House of Correction and Justice Room next door.

1990

Barry Redfern

The location of the next house of correction for Northumberland was at Alnwick, thereby bringing the county justices around full circle in the span of a century. In October 1806 agreement was reached for building a house of correction at Alnwick at a cost of £600. A suitable site was purchased in a lane leading from Green Bat in Alnwick to the Market Place and an architect named David Stephenson, who had previously designed All Saints Church in Newcastle, prepared plans for the new building. A description of the house of correction can be found in a county directory published in 1822.

THE CORRECTION HOUSE. The Correction House stands in a lane leading from the green bat to the Market-place. It was erected in the year 1807, and it contains a workroom, nine cells, and other necessary apartments, with two separate yards for the prisoners, one for each sex. There is also a large room, in which the Justices of the Peace meet regularly once a fortnight to transact business and also at other times when urgent cases require their interference.

(*Description and Historical View of Alnwick*, William Davison 1822, p 217)

The lane referred to by William Davison is still there today. It is a narrow ginnel named Correction House Lane. The remains of Alnwick Correction House are at the back of the council offices in Green Bat but are not marked to identify the old building.

The use of houses of correction continued in the 19th century. But the difference between original purpose and actual use in practice between a gaol and a house of correction was becoming blurred. For example untried prisoners and, in some parts of the country, debtor prisoners were being admitted to houses of correction. The Prison Act of 1865 formally put an end to the distinction between gaols and houses of correction and the term 'prison' came into greater use. The Northumberland institutions remained in use for a few more years but their days were numbered. Huge improvements in transport enabled prisoners to be moved about swiftly, safely and securely. The houses of correction were phased out. National control of penal establishments passed from the local authorities in 1877 to the new Prison Commissioners and a review of the geographical spread of prisons around the country led to widespread closures.

Frederic Hill visited Alnwick in January 1838 and reported, 'The prison of Alnwick is used both as a house of correction and a police prison.' In other words it was, like Tynemouth, being put

Barry Redfern

Frederic Hill.

to use for housing untried prisoners. The chief work there was making mats, teasing horsehair, knitting, sewing, bag making, crushing corn and pounding sand, but it was largely unproductive work. There was only one prisoner, a man, in custody on Hill's arrival at Alnwick. Hill stayed overnight and went back to the house of correction the next morning.

> I am sorry to have to record one gross instance of irregularity, which I was witness to the morning after my arrival. On approaching the prison, I saw a man on the outside, and in the public thoroughfare, shovelling away the snow; the only other person present being a stranger, to whom he was talking. On drawing nigh, it struck me that the man looked very much like the prisoner I had seen the day before and on coming up to him I found that it was really he; and it appeared that it was by the keeper's direction that he was out of the prison and thus occupied.

(3rd Report of the Inspectors Appointed to Visit the Different Prisons of Great Britain, 1838)

The 'keeper' concerned was James Cousins who was soon to be promoted to take charge of the county gaol at Morpeth.

Lock from the gaol at Morpeth.

7. Hanged, drawn and quartered

You are to be drawn on a hurdle to the place of execution, where you are to be hanged by the neck but not until you are dead; for, while you are still living, your body is to be taken down, your bowels torn out and burned before your face; your head then cut off, and your body divided into four quarters, and your head and quarters to be then at the King's disposal; and may Almighty Godhave mercy on your soul.

These chilling words of the death sentence for acts of treason were used twice in the courts of Northumberland in the 18th century. The sentence quoted here makes it clear that the traditional words 'hanged, drawn and quartered' are actually used in the wrong order. Years ago the first part of the sentence was for the offender to be drawn, that is to say dragged along behind a horse, along the road from gaol to gallows. But experience showed that the condemned man arrived at the gallows with little life left in him, which in turn meant that the rest of this dreadful sentence would have little or no effect on the state of fear in the prisoner. The journey to the gallows was then changed to dragging the prisoner along the ground on a wooden hurdle ensuring a rough ride and a painful experience, but arrival at the gallows fully conscious.

In the 18th century no prisoners at Berwick-upon-Tweed or Newcastle upon Tyne received such a sentence. The first prisoners to hear these words at the Northumberland Courts in the 18th century were James Maben and John Samuel in 1744. These two men where convicted of 'counterfeiting the current coin of the realm.' But probably the most important point to make first is that, while Maben and Samuel heard the dreaded sentence pronounced over them by the assize judge Baron Charles Clarke, most of the ignominious suffering in it was remitted. The prisoners were dressed in white, drawn from the Keep in Castlegarth at Newcastle upon Tyne to the gallows at the West Gate on a hurdle and hanged. What method these men and their accomplices used to make the false guineas and shilling pieces is not explained in the surviving papers. But their activity seems to have been mainly based in the Queens Head ale house in the Bigg Market, Newcastle. This leads us to question why Maben and Samuel were tried at the Northumberland Assizes and not those for Newcastle upon Tyne.

Counterfeiting coin or the forging of paper money was, and remains, a very serious offence because of the destabilising effect it can have on the trade and economy of the nation. Undermining the currency 'of the realm' was seen as an offence against the sovereign and therefore ranked as an act of treason. It follows that this offence warranted the special penalty to be hanged, drawn and quartered. Such indictments, which were infrequent, were only tried at the assize courts sitting in the Moot Hall for Northumberland or the Guildhall for Newcastle upon Tyne.

There were some strange twists and turns to this story, beginning in October 1743 when Maben, Samuel and John Dodds were arrested at Newcastle and two other accomplices absconded. Maben, probably understanding only too well the punishment waiting for him at the next assizes, decided to turn King's Evidence against his accomplices. According to the *Newcastle Courant* 29 October 1743, Maben confessed to counterfeiting guineas and shillings, some of which they passed off as genuine. James Leathhead, a schoolmaster, and Thomas Syms, landlord of the Queen's Head, where the tools were kept and the coining was done, had both absconded. Newcastle Corporation offered a reward of 20 guineas each to anyone who arrested them.

Later reports suggested that James Maben might have come from a respectable background, although it is not spelled out clearly. A couple of weeks later a copper plate was found in house of James Leathead the school master. It appeared to be made to print forged English and Scottish bank notes. A few days later an attempt was made by two men and a woman to

Newgate Prison, 1813.

help James Maben escape from Newgate Gaol by forcing the cell window with a crowbar. This was a grave mistake on the part of Maben and marked the end of any hope of saving his life by 'informing' as turning King's Evidence was known.

According to later reports Maben was attacked in the 'dark dungeon' by Dodds and Samuel and forced to withdraw his evidence against his accomplices in a letter to the Mayor of Newcastle. When it came to the trial it was now John Dodds who turned King's Evidence against his colleagues in crime. All involved must have been in a state of panic at the prospect of the punishment for treason to come at the next assizes. Meanwhile, in the same month, the ale-house keeper Thomas Syms was arrested at Berwick but he was not brought south to Newgate Gaol until the following January.

James Leathhead, the schoolmaster, seems to have found a bolt hole somewhere and was not found; but on 27 February 1743/1744 a horse-thief, Thomas Lister, was committed to Morpeth Gaol. He was to have the dubious honour of sharing the gallows with Maben and Samuel a few months later. There matters rested until Baron Charles Clarke, the high court judge, arrived at Newcastle at the end of July 1744 to preside over the

Northumberland Assizes. His colleague, Thomas Burnitt, took the Newcastle upon Tyne Assizes at the Guildhall and it fell to him to deal with John Windram and Alexander Kerr, who had attempted to help James Maben to escape from Newgate gaol. (The woman, 'Isable' Welsh, was not put before the court.). They were ordered to be transported seven years.

At the end of the trials of these 'coiners' at the Moot Hall in Castlegarth, the weight fell on James Maben and John Samuel. Dodds (and his wife) escaped by turning 'King's Evidence'. The ale-house keeper and his wife were cleared and only Maben and Samuel heard the words of the punishment for treason pronounced over them. They must have been mightily relieved to hear news that the sentence was to be 'mitigated' to drawing and hanging.

The horse thief, Thomas Lister, turning this highly public event into a triple execution, joined Maben and Samuel at the gallows. The prisoners were given an uncomfortable ride on a hurdle to the gallows on county land outside the West Gate at Newcastle upon Tyne. The chaplain for the county gaol at Morpeth, the Rev.  George Gordon, attended them. Maben, who the local newspapers described as 'a man of good Education and Abilities, and in some part of his Life, of good Circumstances and Reputation,' showed courage in dealing with death on the gallows, but Samuel was deeply afraid of what was about to happen. The identity of the hangman, as for most of the county executions, is unknown. Maben and Samuel were hanged in the usual way by being turned off a ladder placed against the gallows. The costs of the executions amounted to £15 7s 0d.

The second example of charges of high treason stems from the militia problems of the 18th century. The concept of a local militia is said to be a very old practice in Great Britain. Banding citizens together and training them for local defence was an obligation for freemen in just the same way as taking on parochial duties or joining together to pursue wanted criminals. The militia was an ancestor of the Home Guard of World War II or its successor the Territorial Army, although organised on a county rather than a national basis. In the 16th century the sovereign created the post of Lord Lieutenant in each county, to provide a noble figure to command the militia. The Militia Acts of the 17th century put the militia on a legal footing, but it is the effects of the Militia Act of 1757 that have to be considered here. The need for a local militia arose against the background of the various conflicts of the Seven Years' War with France, and a genuine risk of an invasion on some part of the coastline of the shire counties of England. However, to say it was an unpopular piece of legislation would be a gross understatement.

There were two Militia Acts passed in 1757, the first was 'An Act for the better ordering of the Militia Forces in the several Counties of that Part of Great Britain called England,' (31 Geo. II c25); the second (31 Geo II c26.) was passed to explain the first, make some amendments and provide further guidance. The Lord Lieutenant of each county was appointed to command the militia, with many deputy lieutenants to assist in the day-to-day administration of the force. To qualify for appointment as a deputy lieutenant, the gentlemen had to have an estate worth at least £400 per year or be heir to an estate worth at least £800 per year. Adjutants and sergeants had to be appointed from the regular army or retired soldiers, but retired soldiers who were now ale-house keepers were specifically excluded.

It was in the raising, training and commitment of the force that problems were found. The deputy lieutenants were required to instruct all parish officers in the county to make 'fair and true Lists in Writing,' of all men aged between 18 and 50 in their parishes. The only exemptions were peers, regular soldiers, members of universities, clergymen, teachers of congregations, constables or peace officers, articled clerks, apprentices and seamen.

The full list was to be posted on the door of the parish church. After the number of men to be provided from each parish was settled, the men to serve were chosen by lot and three weeks later were required to attend a meeting and swear the following oath:

I, AB, do sincerely promise and swear to bear true allegiance to His Majesty King George, his Heirs and Successors; and I do swear that I am a Protestant and that I will faithfully serve in the militia within the Kingdom of Great Britain for the Defence of the Realm, during the Time for which I am inrolled, unless I shall be sooner discharged.

(Militia Acts 1757)

The candidate was then committed to the militia for three years. Training days were set for every other Monday from March to October, plus an annual exercise. The Lord Lieutenant was given a measure of flexibility for his county arrangements and to deal with such local rural problems as gathering in the harvest. No pay was given for this service except when the militia was mobilised to deal with the threat of invasion or rebellion, then wages would be paid at regular army rates. The only perquisites of militia service were exemption from parish work and the fact that enrolled members could not be impressed into the regular armed services. Given that 560 able bodied men from Berwick-upon-Tweed, Northumberland and Newcastle upon Tyne were drawn by ballot for this duty, over and above raising forces for the Seven Years' War, it is small wonder that there was dissatisfaction with these laws. The potential for disruption to urban and rural business and trade, and to family life was severe.

There were examples all around the country of this dissatisfaction and resistance to the requirements of the Militia Acts. One early and tragic casualty was Robert Cole, convicted of High Treason in Yorkshire. The presence of soldiers at his execution indicates the high emotions of the time and the precautions the authorities thought necessary.

Hanged at York Monday last [i.e. May 2nd, 1758] Robert Cole one of the Rioters convicted last Assizes of obstructing the Execution of the Militia Act in that County, and George Berry one of the Wensleydale Rioters about corn, the former (i.e. Cole) convicted of High Treason was also drawn and quartered. They both were remarkably penitent, confess'd their being concerned in the said Riots and exhorted their Countrymen to take Warning from their untimely fate. A Party of Sir John Copes Dragoons then in the County, attended the Executions.

Newcastle Journal Saturday 6 May 1758

At the end of the first three-year term, as the time drew near for substantial replacement of men in the militia, the resistance to the militia laws intensified. Entries in the Northumberland Quarter Sessions Order Books show that refusals to register were common, even though it would lead to committal to gaol until the law was obeyed.

In February 1761 the potential for disorder was clearly rising, despite the militia notices being expressed in a conciliatory tone and opening up the path of appeal against inclusion in militia lists. The problem seems to have been an objection to being registered at all rather than being excluded from final selection. Posting lists on church doors confirms the importance of the parish and church as a focal point for district affairs. The surviving lists of meeting places show that inns were used at all places other than the principal county towns.

After some disturbances in County Durham, the *Newcastle Journal* of 28 February reassured readers that no further ballot could be made until the current members had served for three years, and that the current attempt at registration was simply to keep the list of eligible men up to date.

On 7 March 1761 the *Courant* reported that there had been disturbances 'in a riotous manner' at some of the meetings for the militia lists. No details were given but, as will become clear later, there had been a considerable disturbance at Morpeth on 2 March and Belford on 5 March 1761. There was deep apprehension about further serious disorder. Reference was also made back to the riots in Yorkshire and the execution that followed that trouble.

At this time two battalions of the Yorkshire Militia were quartered at Newcastle. Because of the potential for disorder at Hexham, a detachment of the militia was sent to Hexham on Sunday 8 March 1761 to provide a guard for the Militia Meeting to be held at the Sessions Hall. Major Crowe commanded the militia, about 240 of them. The next day, Monday 9 March 1761, was to be a black day in the history of Northumberland. A huge crowd of protestors, perhaps as many as 5,000, armed with pistols, clubs etc. gathered in Hexham Market Place. The militia formed a square around the Sessions Hall to protect the Deputy Lieutenants conducting the preparation of militia lists and balloting, and to ensure that the law was being carried out. As time passed that day the crowd became more and more troublesome. The Riot Act was read at about 2pm, but had no effect in calming or dispersing the crowd. 'Reading the Riot Act' in actual practice meant that a magistrate would read aloud to rioters the following proclamation under the terms of the Riot Act of 1715 (1 Geo I c5).

> **Our Sovereign Lord the King chargeth and commandeth all persons, being assembled, immediately to disperse themselves and peaceably to depart to their habitations or to their lawful business, upon the pains contained in the Act made in the first year of King George the First, for preventing tumults and riotous assemblies. God Save The King.**

The rioters were required to behave well and disperse within one hour. Failure to do so would render the individual guilty of felony and the punishment for a felon in the 18th century was death.

Hexham Market Place, early 19th century.

The crowd ignored the proclamation and became more excited and violent. They pressed on the militia lines and in the course of this disorder a soldier was shot with his own weapon and an ensign was wounded by a pistol shot. The ensign died the following day. The press reports of the day say, 'the Magistrates were obliged and did give the command to fire.' The militia opened fire on the rioters and it is said that 51 died and above 300 were wounded. The crowd of rioters rushed for cover in the streets leading away from the market place. The home places listed for the dead help to give some idea of where the rioters had come from – Hexham, Slaley, Broomley, Bywell, Prudhoe, Blanchland, Crooked Oak, Newburn, Fourstones, Newbrough, Haydon Bridge, Ryal, Throckley, Heddon on the Wall, Chollerton, Stamfordham and Walwick.

The local newspapers carried reports about the Hexham riot and the thanks of the Deputy Lieutenants to the Yorkshire Militia. The following example is from the *Newcastle Journal*. It seems that rumours were being circulated after the riot that Sir Lancelot Allgood of Nunwick had offered the Yorkshire Militia first £50 then £100 to fire on the rioters at Hexham Market Place. Sir Lancelot denied this as a 'false and villainous' allegation.

> The DEPUTY LIEUTENANTS; JUSTICES OF THE PEACE and other gentlemen of the County of Northumberland take this publick Method of tendering their Thanks to Col. DUNCOMB, Major CROWE and the rest of the OFFICERS; and also to the PRIVATE MEN in the two Yorkshire Battalions of Militia now quartered at Newcastle for their ready & effectual Service in suppressing a riotous & unlawful Assembly of the People at Hexham on Monday last.
> *Newcastle Journal* 12 March 1761

WHEREAS some among the RIOTERS, that met at Hexham last Monday, to oppose the Execution of the MILITIA LAWS of this country, did inform the others and have been propagating it ever since, that I Sir LANCELOT ALLGOOD did offer the Soldiers Fifty, and afterwards One Hundred

Pounds, if they would level their pieces well, and fire: – In Justice therefore to my own character, I do hereby declare that the said Report is false and villainous; nor did I offer any Sum of Money whatsoever to the said Soldiers, in order to induce them to fire. And I do hereby promise to pay to any Person who shall convict the Author, or Authors of the said Report, the sum of Twenty Guineas, on such Conviction as aforesaid

March 12 1761. L. ALLGOOD

Newcastle Journal Saturday 14 March 1761 (extract)

Recriminations about the militia opening fire on the rioters were also met by a letter from an unnamed person to the *Newcastle Journal* the following week. It gave greater detail of the provocative and life threatening behaviour of the rioters and reassured the public that the firing had been stopped at the earliest possible time. Sir Lancelot Allgood continued to proclaim his innocence.

To the PUBLISHERS of the NEWCASTLE JOURNAL

Gentlemen,

You are desired to rectify a Mistake in the Article of your Account of the Riot at Hexham, in your last Week's Paper ... it appears the Numbers that Day assembled at Hexham, was considerably upwards of 5,000. We cannot help expressing our surprise here at the Liberty taken by the Publisher of a certain News-Paper, intitled St. James Chronicle; wherein he taxes the Officers and Soldiers with unrelenting Barbarity, in continuing the Fire after all Resistance was over. So far from this, I can assure him, from the best Authority, that greater Forbearance never was known among the best disciplined Troops: That for Upwards of four Hours they bore with the greatest patience the most opprobrious Insults from the Mob, and received no Orders to fire till they made the most daring Attack upon the Left of the Line, and actually broke it, wrested some Bayonets of the Men's Firelocks, and seized a piece belonging to one of the private Men and shot him dead: At this Time an Officer also fell. The Men in an instant formed, and the fire became general, and many of those who made the rash Attempt paid dearly for their Temerity. It is but Justice due to this Handful of brave Men, to say, that the firing became an absolute Act of Necessity and Self Preservation; for had it been delayed one Moment longer, it is most certain it would have proved fatal to themselves. The Minute Resistance ceased, the Officers omitted no endeavours to stop the Fire; and those Endeavours instantly met with the desired Success ...

Newcastle Journal Saturday 21 March 1761

The deaths of so many people at this riot brought an end to major disorder, but there was still deep concern and anxiety throughout the county. The justices at the Northumberland Quarter Sessions abandoned their usual pattern of sittings of the sessions and met by adjournment every week for several months. In the Northumberland County Record Office there are some fascinating letters written during the week following the riot by Lady Jane Allgood of Nunwick to her husband Sir Lancelot Allgood. He was a senior magistrate and a member of the Grand Jury for Northumberland and was spending most of his time at Newcastle at sittings of the adjourned quarter sessions. A few short extracts give an intimate view of a woman of strong character, determination and with a sense of humour, and also some indication of the impact of the riot on country life.

Correspondence from Lady Allgood to her husband Sir Lancelot Allgood March 1761 after the Hexham Riots (extracts)

(NB there was no punctuation in Lady Allgood's letters)

My Dear

... I have sent Wm with this as I thought you would want cloaths ... Robt Allgood ... came yesterday to defend me as he said but I told him he looked so frighted I rather thought he meant I was to defend him Jack Baty has got four of my father's old Blunderbusses out he says he knows the good they have done they are as rusty as if they had been taken out of the river I surveyed all their war like accoutrements last night & laughed most immoderately they put me so much in mind of Falstaffs company it has afforded us a great deal of diversion ... Mr Beaumont staid all night part of four body guard tonight is Will Coulson of Simonburn & Joe Cowen I told Beaumont I would appoint him Capt of the guard tonight his bulk will best suit Falstaffs

My Dear

I have just received your kind letter & in the first place I beg you won't let your noble courage be dismayed consider you have God your King your Country (that is the valuable part of it) & its laws to defend you against a parcell of Banditti unarmed hot headed runagadess thank God mine has never failed me even when they trailed me out of the House telling me it was for my own safety that they were coming to burn the House they carried me through the wood to the gate by John Ridley's wher I stopt & asked what was the matter I was not afraid if they were all surrounding me I knew God would protect me & he was all sufficient let who would be against me & just came by at the time half a hund'd like so many thievish dogs whip'd to their Kennel I lectured them most stoutly told them they deserved what they met with would not take my advice who had told them what they must expect for I had sent up the day before to let them know their assembling themselves in that manner would be deemed rebellion & must be treated as rebels & if any of our Tenants or whoever they were that lived upon any part of our estate went with the rebellious crew they were none belonging to them should have habitation here again & this morning I have sent to tell them if they don't behave themselves quietly & decently as loyal subjects ought to do in a christian county they shall have a regiment of soldiers to drive them like a flock of sheep to slaughter & teach them what it is to go to fight because they wont learn to fight like a parcell of wild Irish as they are ...

& am My Dear Your Affect Wife

Jane Allgood

Nunwick

Friday night

(probably written Friday evening 13 March 1761)

(Northumberland Record Office Access No. ZAL/40/12)

There is a reference in these letters to Lady Allgood asking the local vicar to preach against the rebellion. This appears to be in line with a tactic adopted by the county magistrates. The magistrates later expressed their gratitude at the sessions.

Northumberland Quarter Sessions Order Books.1753 -1763

Order made at Midsummer Sessions 31st July 1761

This court taking into consideration the unhappy and desperate Riots which lately disturbed the peace of this county doth with the Concurrence and Approbation of the Grand Jury give the Thanks of the County in this public Manner to the several Clergymen of the Church of England and Ministers or

Teachers of the Dissenting Congregations within the said County for their Laudable Attention to the Tranquillity and Happiness of the County manifested by their seasonable Discourses from the Pulpit and elsewhere to impress on the minds of their hearers a due sense of the Heinousness and evil Tendency of the Crime of Fomenting or engaging in Riots and Tumults to the Disturbance of the public peace and particularly to the Rev. Mr John Brown DD and Vicar of Newcastle upon Tyne The Rev. Mr Totton Lecturer at Hexham and the Rev. Mr Stoddart Vicar of Cholerton for their able performances delivered from the pulpit on that subject and for publishing the same by means whereof they became more extensively useful.

(Northumberland Record Office Access No. QSO 9)

In the days after the riot, the county magistrates were issuing warrants for the arrest of people believed to have taken part in the disturbances. The sessions' records contain many notes of payments to High Constables and Petty Constables for the costs of making arrests and taking prisoners to gaol. The Yorkshire Militia continued to play their part in preventing further trouble by providing escorts for prisoners. Two prisoners who were to play prominent roles in later events were Peter Patterson (or Paterson), aged about 74 years from Shilvington, and William Elder of Rock in Northumberland. It is unfortunate that the case papers, that is to say the sworn evidence in the form of depositions, for Patterson and Elder, and others tried at the next assizes, have not survived and there is little left to make a proper assessment of exactly what Patterson and Elder did to warrant the extremely serious charges laid against them. The archive of State Papers at the Public Record Office shows that the Deputy Lieutenants of Northumberland reported, at great speed, the riots at Hexham to the Secretary of State, who was in a position to write on the matter on 12 March 1761 before referring the matter to King George III the following day.

There was a swift response to the request for assistance from a regiment of light horse.

This week three troops of the Royal Forester Light Dragoons came into this Town from York; and we hear they are to be quartered at Hexham, Morpeth, and in this neighbourhood.

Newcastle Journal 21 March 1761

By 24 April 1761, the county authorities at Northumberland had supplied to the Secretary of State (now John, Earl of Bute, appointed 25 March 1761) a list of the names of prisoners in custody following the riots, along with copies of the sworn informations taken against them. Bute referred the papers to the Attorney General for consideration. On 25 May 1761,

Bute wrote to Philip Cartaret Webb, Solicitor to the Treasury saying that the Attorney General had reported insufficient evidence in the early reports of the riots in Northumberland and recommended that an agent be sent to procure more information. A similar action had been taken in the case of the Yorkshire rioters.

On 9 July Bute sent the Attorney General the further evidence collected by the agent sent into Northumberland. None of this material has survived, but based on that evidence Bills of Indictment were drawn up alleging High Treason by Paterson, Elder and a man called George Irwin. A number of other men were to be charged with riotously and treasonably opposing the extension of the militia laws. All were to be tried at the Northumberland Assizes.

The Northumberland Assizes first opened on Monday 27 July 1761 but, after the bills of indictment were reviewed by the Grand Jury, all prisoners charged with offences arising out of the riots were stood down for trial at a special adjourned sitting of the Northumberland Assizes at the Moot Hall, Newcastle beginning on 17 August. Between the two sittings, the judges left Newcastle for Carlisle to clear the gaols of Cumberland and Westmoreland, then on to Lancaster for the Lancashire Assizes. A week before the trials of the rioters were due to begin, the Secretary of State wrote a significant letter to Mr Norton, the barrister acting for the Crown, advising him to speak privately to the judges and recommend that they should delay the executions of those convicted of High Treason to allow time for the King to consider 'how far it may be proper to extend His Royal Mercy to them.'

The Adjourned Northumberland Assizes were held in the Moot Hall on Monday and Tuesday 17 and 18 August 1761. The serious and unusual nature of the matters for trial is revealed in two ways here, first the size of the Grand Jury who had first considered the Bills of Indictment: the jury had comprised of six baronets, three knights and 35 gentlemen of Northumberland; and secondly, the trials of the rioters were presided over by two High Court Judges sitting together, the Honourable Henry Bathurst and Sir Richard Lloyd. The 'Prison Calendar' for the rioters has survived and is preserved in the Public Record Office (Access ASSI 44/76). It is an unusual, impressive and specially prepared document measuring three feet by two and half feet. The script is written in more than one colour with flourishes and ornaments. It is a work of calligraphic art and ought not to be hidden away. Listed on the document are the Privy Council, the Judges, the Grand Jurors of Northumberland, the Sheriffs, Alexander Collingwood and William Gibson (Under Sheriff), the Coroners, Thomas Mayor and Nicholas Brown, the High Constables, the Bailiffs of the Liberties and the Bailiffs of the Hundreds.

These details are followed by a list of the prisoners, Peter Patterson, William Elder and 14 others charged with High Treason by Riotously and Treasonably opposing Enforcement of the Militia Laws. It is the Indictments, Minute Book and Gaol Book that begin to reveal some of the detail that was lost with sworn depositions against these men. There has been some confusion by writers describing the Hexham Riots about the links between Peter Patterson, William Elder and the events at Hexham on 9 March 1761. There was no allegation made in these records that Patterson or Elder had even been present at Hexham that day. The text of the indictment against Patterson was as follows.

HIGH TREASON

Peter Patterson, Late of Shilvington, yeoman (endorsed 'Puts Guilty') subject of our said Sovereign Lord George III wickedly devising and intending to disturb the peace on 2nd March 1 Geo III at Morpeth in the County of Northumberland traiterously compassed imagined and intended to levy war and insurrection against the King with aforesaid arms at Morpeth with a great Multitude of riotous and tumultuous persons whose names are as yet unknown, to a great number to wit to the number of five hundred and upwards, being armed and arrayed in a warlike manner, that is to say with Pistols, Swords, Scythes, Staves, Clubs and other Offensive and defensive weapons and being then and there unlawfully, falsely, and traiterously assembled and gathered together most wickedly and traiterously prepared, waged and levied public war against our said Lord the King, his superior and undoubted Lord, contrary to the Duty of his allegiance against the Peace of our said Lord the King, his Crown and Dignity against the Form of the Statute in the said case made and proved.

(The margin of the indictment is endorsed 'A TRUE BILL')

(PRO Access No. ASSI 44/76)

So Peter Patterson was involved in the troubles at the meeting at the Sessions Hall at Morpeth on 2 March 1761, as listed above in the *Courant* report of 21 February 1761, and not at Hexham. The *Courant* report of 7 March 1761, as given earlier, had indicated that there had been disorder at the meetings but there was no depth to the report.

A similar situation occurs with William Elder, the indictment against him, in identical terms, alleged the 'levying of war against the King' at Belford on 5 March 1761, which is when the meeting for Balmbrough Ward was to be held at William Bugg's (the Innkeeper of Belford). Given that Shilvington, the home of Patterson, is close to Morpeth, and Rock, the home of William Elder, is not far from Belford and Balmbrough, it makes more sense to conclude that each man was involved in, what were for them, more local demonstrations.

When the day came for the trials a barrister named Thomas Gale was appointed to defend Peter Patterson, William Elder and others. While bills for High Treason had been found against 16 prisoners, the King's Counsel for the Crown, Mr Norton, made some changes and adjustments to the charges with the consent of the judges. William Elder was found guilty of high treason at Belford and Patterson guilty of high treason at Morpeth. George Irwin was cleared of high treason at Morpeth. Three others indicted for high treason at the Hexham riots were found not guilty and the remaining prisoners were either acquitted or convicted of minor offences and fined or imprisoned for one week.

So, strictly speaking, no one was convicted of High Treason for involvement in the Hexham Riots. The death of 51 people in the Market

Place at Hexham was a terrible penalty in itself.

Peter Patterson and William Elder had the dreaded sentence for High Treason pronounced over them. This is how it was recorded in the Gaol Book.

Newcastle and Northumberland Gaol Book 1761

PETER PATTERSON AND WILLIAM ELDER

Attainted of High Treason. To be drawn upon an Hurdle to the place of Execution on Wednesday the thirteenth day of September next and then and there severally hanged by the Neck, To be severally cut down alive and have their Entrails taken out and burnt before their faces, To have their heads severed from their bodies, And their bodies afterwards severally divided into four Quarters And their heads and Quarters disposed of at his Majesty's pleasure.

(PRO Access No. ASSI 42/5)

The *Newcastle Journal* of Saturday 29 August 1761 reported that the executions had been deferred until 5 October.

Towards the end of September 1761, the Secretary of State wrote to the Earl of Northumberland with the decision of the King. Peter Patterson would be executed on 5 October, in the hope that this punishment would deter others from committing similar crimes. William Elder would be held in prison until the King had time for further consideration of his case.

Seventy-four-year-old Peter Patterson was executed at Fair Moor, Morpeth. He behaved with a becoming decency.

A man named John Dawson of Brunton in his diary transcribed many years ago for the Surtees Society recorded more detail.

DIARY OF JOHN DAWSON OF BRUNTON

1761, October 4th Sunday,

Accounts come of Peter Patterson to be hanged to-morrow or Tuesday

1761, October 5th, Monday

At home all day

1761, October 6th, Tuesday

Peter Patterson was hanged, yesterday, at Morpeth on account of the riot that happened there about eight months ago. Peter Patterson was a leader of the mob. In this riot Mr Fenwick of Bywell got his head broke. Nichol Waugh who came from Morpeth this morning gives the following account about Peter Patterson viz.: -

That he was with him on Sunday evening last when he was chearful. That yesterday morning he took his leave of Peter. That Peter died very penitent, That when he was hung up, the rope either slipt or broke and so he fell. That after he was recovered he was hung up a second time; then cut down; his head cut off; his heart taken out and thrown into the fire; then his quarters were cut across but not cut off. He is supposed to have died worth between three and four thousand pounds. That excepting an annuity to his wife, he has left all his fortune to his mistress. Mr Brown of Kirkharle is trustee for the woman and children. Nichol Waugh gave me the above account at my own front door at Brunton. Peter Patterson was about 74 years of age.

(Surtees Society, 1814, I, North Country Diaries II)

Despite all that had occurred, the work of enforcing the provisions of the Militia Act had to continue. There were no reports of trouble at the future meetings. In the *Newcastle Journal* the same week was the final report on William Elder, who had spent six months in custody awaiting his trial and a further 12 months in the county gaol awaiting his pardon.

The Assizes ended on Wednesday [12 August]. For the County of Northumberland, William Elder, who was tried last assizes, found guilty of High Treason, received Sentence of Death, and continued in prison since then, discharged on his Recognisance, having receiv'd his Majesty's free Pardon.

Newcastle Journal Saturday 14 August 1763

8. Justice at Berwick-upon-Tweed

> The Mayor, Recorder, and Justices, have by their charter, a power
> to hold general and quarter-sessions of the peace within the
> borough, for the trial of petty felonies, trespasses, and other
> misdemeanours. They have also a power of holding a general gaol
> delivery for the trial of capital felonies; and such as are capitally
> convicted at these trials are executed within the borough, it having
> a gallows for that purpose. The sessions, or court of gaol delivery,
> cannot be held without the Mayor and Recorder, who when,
> elected into office, continue Justices of the Peace for life within the
> borough.
>
> (*History of Berwick-upon-Tweed*, James Fuller 1799)

This is the unique feature of Berwick-upon-Tweed in the context of
the 18th century and the subject of this book. The itinerant Judges
of Assize did not visit Berwick-upon-Tweed to clear the gaols. The
charter for the town permitted the Mayor, Recorder and Justices to take on
that task themselves when necessary. So, from time to time, a heavy
responsibility fell on the Recorder, as the legally qualified person presiding
over the general gaol delivery, and on the Mayor of the borough, as the
principal magistrate. The quarter sessions for the borough were held at the
usual times, Christmas (January), Easter (April), Midsummer (July) and
Michaelmass (October). General gaol delivery for the more serious crimes,
usually capital offences, was held when required and occasionally may have
been held before or after a sitting of the quarter sessions in the town hall.

Exclusion from the normal Assize Circuit around the boroughs, cities and
shire counties of England and Wales had its roots firstly in the history of
military control, secondly the independence of the borough and thirdly in

the sheer isolation of Berwick. It was an ancient borough at the northern tip of England on the Scottish border, populated by a rugged, independently minded set of people. Travel there by the judges would have been difficult and dangerous in the early days. Transporting prisoners and witnesses to the assizes at Newcastle upon Tyne at that time were out of the question for the same reasons. The officials and people of Berwick took on the responsibility of administering criminal justice for centuries without the help of high court judges to preside over their senior courts. Life and death decisions about the serious crimes rested with them.

The powers of the officials of Berwick, as used in the 18th century, stemmed from a charter of James I in 1603. The rights, responsibilities and privileges under the charter created a corporate structure of the Mayor and four Bailiffs to govern the town that, although not a county in its own right, was distinct and separate from the shire counties of Northumberland and Durham. The quarter sessions and general gaol delivery were presided over by the Recorder (a legally qualified advocate), the Mayor and not less than three justices of the peace. The jury system was the same as elsewhere, a Grand Jury to review indictments and a Petit Jury to decide innocence or guilt.

Improvements in transport in the 19th century made travel easier in Northumberland. The government was preparing for the reform of municipal corporations. Against that background, in 1833 Robert Ingham, Recorder of Berwick-upon-Tweed, in evidence to Parliamentary Select Committee expressed some reservations about the fairness of an intensely parochial system of criminal justice in the borough. He believed it was desirable that all trials of capital offences take place before the King's judges in the adjoining county (that is to say Northumberland); he also felt that the small population of Berwick restricted choice for juries. There was a potential conflict of interest arising from the growth of associations for the prosecution of felons, where residents and tradesmen gathered resources together to pursue felons and pay the costs of prosecutions. Members of such associations found themselves sitting on juries for cases funded by their organisations. (Parliamentary Papers Vol. XIII 1833)

Local gaol delivery at Berwick-upon-Tweed was brought to an end by an act of Parliament in 1842 (5 & 6 Vict. c38). Local quarter sessions continued in the borough, but the more serious cases were committed for trial at the Northumberland Assizes at the Moot Hall Newcastle upon Tyne.

Every town and borough needed a building to hold prisoners and W.W. Tomlinson related a story of what must have been a very unpleasant gaol at Berwick-upon-Tweed in the 16th century.

> A Scotsman, for walking along the walls of Berwick from the highe mount to Roaring Megge's mount, prying and looking verie circumspectlie about him as he walked, on 1st May 1593 was committed by John Carey to 'Haddock's Hole' which is described by the Mayor of Berwick as 'a vyle, fylthe pryson appoynted for thieves and murderers.' This prison was no doubt a type of many others in the county, in which the bold moss troopers languished 'sick and like to die.'
>
> (*Life in Northumberland in the 16th Century*, William Weaver Tomlinson 1897, page 232.)

John Scott, writing in 1888 (*History of Berwick-upon-Tweed* by John Scott 1888, page 436), said that the site 'Haddock's Hole' is unknown, but it was one of three gaols at Berwick in about 1600. Another was the 'House in the Wall' near the Drum Flag Staff on the south west corner of the wall on the water side. The third gaol was in the Tol-booth or Town Hall. It is said that there were three town halls put up on the same site at the foot of Marygate in the centre of Berwick. The third town hall, dating from 1754, with a magnificent clock steeple, is a distinguished building in a cramped site in the centre of the road. It contains the former courtroom and gaol; the building is open to the public from spring to autumn and well worth a visit.

The borough gaol was on the top floor of the town hall above the courtroom. John Howard, the 18th century prison reformer, visited Berwick in 1776, 1779 and 1782. In his book he placed the report on Berwick-upon-Tweed Gaol next to Northumberland and commented on the fact that the borough was not in any assize circuit. The gaoler at Berwick on Howard's first visit was John Richardson, who was succeeded by John Hill; they were paid a salary of £16 per annum. No gaol fees were charged to prisoners except debtors who were not freemen, in which case a fee of two shillings and sixpence was payable to the gaoler. The allowance (feeding) for prisoners was two and a half pence per day, except for freemen debtors who were allowed fourpence per day plus coals. The garnish (a fee payable to existing prisoners by a new prisoner) was one shilling and fourpence. There was no chaplain. A surgeon would only be called on application to the magistrates. John Howard was not impressed; his report on the gaol was short and to the point.

BERWICK

THIS gaol is part of the grand town-hall, which was finished in 1754, and has a fine steeple: the only one in town. The four rooms or cells on the ground-floor are damp and prisoners are not put into them, but over the hall, where there are two long rooms, or galleries, and seven other rooms, sizeable, but dirty. No court: the debtors are permitted to walk on the leads: no water: no sewer. Clauses against spirituous liquors, and the act for preserving the health of prisoners, not hung up. The gaoler told me he went to the gaol thrice a day: at nine, one and eight.

(*The State of the Prisons* by John Howard 4th Edition 1792)

In the next two descriptions of Berwick Gaol, published within seven years of each other, it is hard to accept that the writers are describing the same gaol examined by John Howard, and in the first John Fuller, with his high flown language, seems preoccupied with what can be seen from the gaol rather than the condition of the prisoners.

The upper flat (of the Town Hall) is occupied as a common gaol, and is perhaps the most healthy and pleasant one in the Kingdom, This owing to its many large windows, from which the prisoners enjoy excellent views of the Town, the German Ocean, Bamburgh Castle and Holy Island … these captivating objects tend to soothe the mind, and to alleviate the sufferings of confinement, they, at the same time, hold out the inestimable blessings of unrestrained Liberty – the birth right of and generally the reward of virtue, industry, and honesty; but the indolent, the fraudulent, the robber, and the murderer are not entitled to the heaven-borne enjoyment.

(*History of Berwick-upon-Tweed*, John Fuller, 1799, page 180)

We have an excellent Town-hall & Steeple with a capital clock which Chimes the quarters. This Hall contains a large Guild-hall, where the Courts & Sessions are holden. The Jail is also in this Hall which is kept remarkably clean by Mr William Brown* the jailor and is a fine airy situation with a pipe of fresh water in it. All prisoners, both debtors and felons, are maintained at the expense of the Corporation. It is more like a gentlemen's gallery than a

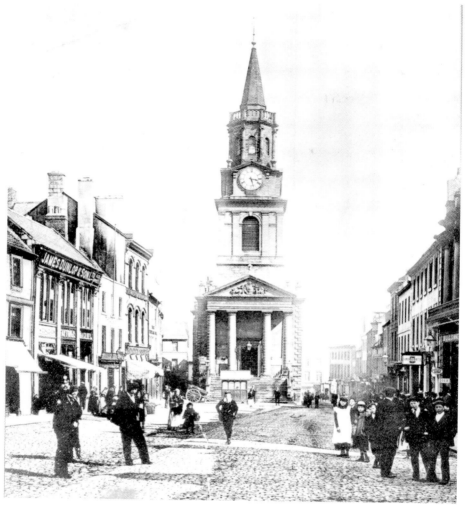

Berwick Town Hall around 1900.

Jail, only the confinement is not very agreeable.

It would be well if the Town would erect a House of Correction in this place, and cause some of these people to work (who care not for the jail) and live on their own earnings the time of their confinement, it would cause them to behave better in future and be a saving for to the Corporation. There has not been an Execution here since the year 1760, therefore we have no hangman.

(*A Directory and Concise History of Berwick-upon-Tweed*, James Good, 1806, page 73)

(* Mr William Brown, Jailor, is also listed as the Innkeeper of the Berwick-upon-Tweed Arms, High Street, Berwick.)

The famous Quakers, Joseph John Gurney and his sister Elizabeth Fry, who were so active in prison reform following the practice of John Howard, visited Berwick Gaol on 26 August 1818.

BERWICK BOROUGH GAOL

Nothing can be much more defective than this small prison. It consists of two large boarded rooms in the upper story of the Court-house; one for debtors, the other for criminals – a simple wooden door between them.

Connected with these day-rooms is a small range of sleeping cells. The whole prison is so exceedingly insecure that the criminals cannot be permitted to make use of their day-room except in the presence of the jailer. Thus they are almost constantly confined in their sleeping-cells. Nor is this provision deemed sufficient: when their cases are bad they are chained to the wall. The injustice and barbarity of such a mode of confinement are too conspicuous to require a comment. Neither criminals nor debtors have any airing-ground. The prison allowance is sixpence per day. No clothing is allowed, nor is there any provision for medical attendance or religious instruction.

(*Notes on a Visit made to some of the Prisons in Scotland and the North of England in Company with Elizabeth Fry*, Joseph John Gurney, 1819, page 17.)

The conditions in the gaol continued to deteriorate and 20 years later, in January 1838, when Frederic Hill carried out the first government inspection of Berwick Gaol, he submitted to the Secretary of State a scathing report on every aspect of the prison. It was a very long, intensely detailed document in which Hill did not hesitate to draw attention to the reason why no money was being spent on improving the building. Hill began his report as follows:

BERWICK-UPON-TWEED

Population, including that of Spittle and Tweedmouth, about 14,000.

The prison at Berwick has long been noted as a very bad one; and it appears fully to have deserved its reputation. The evils, however, have been much mitigated of late owing to a considerable decrease in the number of prisoners, especially of those convicted of smuggling. Until within the last two years or three years the prison was often much crowded; and as young and old, males and females, met together in the same day room, with sleeping rooms opening into it, scenes of the greatest profligacy were, I understand, of frequent occurrence … when there are prisoners of different sexes at the same time, illicit intercourse is probably sometimes carried on, the arrangements of the prison, and the absence of the keeper during the greater part of the day (for he does not reside on the spot), affording facilities for it … The prison is formed out of the upper story of the town-house, and is constructed entirely of wood; the partitions, floors and ceilings being all of the same material. It is a matter of wonder to me, that the place has not long ago been destroyed by fire; and if a fire could have taken place without sacrifice of the inmates, such an event would have been fortunate. Great age cannot be pleaded as an excuse for the bad construction of this prison, for there are people still alive who remember its being built … The windows look upon the street, and intercourse goes on with the outside, though to a less degree than formerly, owing to the erection of hopper blinds before some of the windows.

(Third Report of the Inspectors Appointed to Visit the Different Prisons of Great Britain, 1838)

These are strong and uncompromising words, and it is also interesting to note how this professional, Frederic Hill, looked at the windows of the gaol in such a different way from John Fuller. Hill did not see a magnificent view, only the potential for trouble through improper communication with people in the street. Hill remarks later in his report under the heading 'Discipline', 'The most frequent prison offence that came to the knowledge of the keeper is getting supplies of food and spirits through the windows.' Hill noted that the annual salaries of the officials were, the keeper £70, the chaplain £20 and the surgeon £10.

Hill expressed with great force and clarity his final conclusion that Berwick should be provided with a new prison.

It is very desirable that no time should be lost in abandoning this bad prison, and in providing a good one in its stead. The old freemen (who divide among themselves a considerable portion of the borough funds, and who therefore have a strong interest in preventing any outlay for such a purpose as building a prison) admit, I believe, their liability (under the provisions of their charter) to keep up a gaol, but they contend that they are not bound to provide a house of correction. And there has been some idea of the erection of two separate buildings, namely a gaol by the Corporation and a house of correction by the inhabitants at large. I hope however that this plan will not be persisted in, as I look upon the distinction between a gaol and a house of correction as artificial and unnecessary, and not likely to endure.

(Third Report of the Inspectors Appointed to Visit the Different Prisons of Great Britain, 1838)

The freemen resisted this recommendation as they felt no liability or responsibility to provide a second prison in the borough. They relied on the wording of the town charter that said 'We (etc) do grant to the said Mayor (etc) that they may within the said borough (etc) have one Prison or Gaol for the prisoning or keeping of all & singular prisoners within the said borough (and so forth).' Frederic Hill felt that they were simply hiding behind the wording of an ancient charter to avoid spending money that would otherwise be divided amongst the freemen of the town.

Before leaving Berwick, Frederic Hill left a long list of recommendations for improving the existing gaol, and to the credit of the Berwick authorities, Hill was soon assured by letter from the Under Sheriff, Mr Weddell, that all the recommendations had been carried out.

The authorities at Berwick had been exploring the possibilities of sharing gaol facilities with a part of Durham, called North Durham, which consisted of about 70 square miles of land that bordered onto the borough of Berwick-upon-Tweed, but no agreement was reached. This critical assessment of the local gaol by Hill was to prove to be the catalyst for change. Over the next decade Berwick-upon-Tweed came to terms with the challenge of following the example of their neighbours, Northumberland, Newcastle upon Tyne and Durham, by taking steps to provide a new prison for the town. Had they known how short the life of the new prison would be and the changes that were being made in local government, criminal jurisdiction and, eventually, policing, one wonders what the worthy burgesses of Berwick would have decided to do. A new gaol was opened in Wallace Green on Monday 26 November, 1849 with William Whinna as governor.

Berwick at the beginning of the 19th century.

The following weekend, Saturday 8 December 1849, the *Berwick Advertiser* carried a long article about the old and new gaols at Berwick, including an outline plan of two of the three floors of the new building and an etching of the outside. The journalist who wrote this article appears to have had deep reservations about the whole project. He expressed doubts about the location, the design, the space available for prisoners and the cost. The new building was designed by Mr Brown of Edinburgh, the government architect of prisons, and built by Adam Young of Kelso at a cost of £7,460 6s 6d.

On the ground floor there was a court room measuring 26ft by 20ft, airing yards, reception rooms for prisoners, toilets, cells and living space for the matron. On the next floor above the court room was a chapel of the same dimensions, two rooms for debtors, cells and living space and offices for the keeper; and above that on the top floor were five cells. The journalist expressed the opinion that the justices already had an adequate courtroom in a more convenient place and the chapel was an extravagance.

The same report said that the greatest number of prisoners at one time in the Town Hall Gaol at Berwick had been 38, with as many as 25 at one time for smuggling whisky. But from time to time there were no prisoners in the gaol. The report also included some fascinating anecdotes about escapes from the Town Hall Gaol. Everything in the prison was made of wood, which, apart from the danger of fire, rendered it vulnerable to attack. Some prisoners on one occasion prised up some floor boards forced their way through the plaster into the justices' room and dropped up to 17 feet to the floor to make their escape. On another occasion, a debtor prisoner named John Brown, a former sailor, was walking on the lead flats of the Town Hall roof when he took his chance, and one might say his life in his hands, and jumped from the roof to the top of a passing cartload of hay. John Brown survived the jump of about 40 feet but broke his leg getting down from the cart to the ground and was seized and taken back to gaol.

In 1816 there was a blind man, well known in the borough, who had been imprisoned for some six years for debt arising out of a dispute about property. The man was about 54 and had been blind since he was three years of age. He had instructed a solicitor to try and secure his release under some legislation about debtors, but felt that the lawyer was not getting on with the task to his satisfaction. At that time workmen were repairing the roof of the Town Hall and had long ladders reaching up to the roof about 40 feet or more from the pavement. Given his blindness the man was not thought to be a risk and was allowed on the roof; he climbed down the ladder to the ground unaided and made off. He visited his solicitor who warned him about the consequences of escape and the report concludes, 'He thence speedily hastened to his old domicile. Having rung the bell he was admitted, to the no small wonder and surprise of the jailer, who until the return of his prisoner was ignorant of his escape.'

In 1819, two boys from Edinburgh, in custody for fraud, forced their way into the steeple and used the bell ropes to climb down to the street, all the time encumbered by heavy irons. Their mistake was to ask a country blacksmith to remove the irons. They were quickly returned to Berwick Gaol.

One final escape story relates to an Irishman named Alexander Macdougall, who was a prisoner at the Town Hall in 1836. He and other prisoners were working picking oakum and he saved enough of the material each day to make a rope that he wound around his body under his clothing to conceal it from the jail staff. When the rope reached a length of 50 feet

Macdougall made his escape by lowering himself from the roof.

In 1877, less than 30 years after the new borough gaol had opened, control of prisons passed from local government to the new Prison Commissioners. More than 30 small prisons were closed including the borough prison at Wallace Green, Berwick. Today the old 19th century borough gaol for Berwick forms part of the Council Offices.

There were only four civil executions at Berwick between 1672 and 1823. The first was on 24 August 1672 when John Smithson, the Vicar of Berwick-upon-Tweed, was hanged for the murder of his wife Sarah. The borough gallows was said to have been near to the castle. Smithson had been appointed as Vicar in 1664. Not much detail has survived about this crime but John Scott quoted a useful extract from local records.

> On October 2nd, 1762, whereas by the horrid murder which Mr John Smithson, late Vicar, committed upon his own late wife, Sarah Roseden, (sister of Roseden, lessee of the Rectory) of which inhuman murder he was found guilty, condemned and executed for the same according to law, all his tenements, lands, goods and chattels, whatsoever at the time of the felony committed are, by his Majesty's Charter granted to this Burgh, forfeit to this town.

(*Berwick-upon-Tweed, the History of the Town and Guild*, John Scott, 1888)

It is possible to draw to together a selection of examples from the borough quarter sessions records books and other sources and build up a picture of crime and punishment at Berwick-upon-Tweed in the 18th century – something loosely akin to a diary that will include two more of the executions, beginning in 1715 when a gentleman faced the possibility of punishment at the gallows.

Berwick-upon-Tweed Quarter Sessions Order Book 1694-1726

Decimo Octavo Die Januarii 1715 (18th January 1715/1716)

John Carr, gent, indicted for murder of John Miller, gent, guilty of manslaughter pleaded benefit of the statute, the said John Carr was burnt on the hand and released subject to recognisances.

(Northumberland Record Office. Access No. C.8/1)

John Carr escaped punishment by pleading Benefit of Clergy by reading a test piece from the Holy Bible. The branding, usually on the left thumb, with a letter 'F' prevented the man claiming the benefit a second time. John Carr 'Gentleman' was undoubtedly a very fortunate man to escape punishment with just branding, painful though that may have been. A few years later when the Transportation Act of 1717/18 came into effect he would, in addition to branding, have been transported to America or the West Indies probably for life.

In 1729 there was an example of the oldest profession in the world being practised at Berwick:

Berwick-upon-Tweed Quarter Sessions Book 1727 -1745.

Presentment of the Grand Jury Septo die (seventh day) Jun(e) 1729

We present – Margaret Campbell being reputed a woman of ill fame in this place Strolling about this town having no certain habitation.

Northumberland Record Office Access No. C.8/2

'Presentment' meant reporting a problem to the justices at the quarter sessions and it is not clear what the justices decided to do about Margaret Campbell. If she was from outside the borough she could be moved on as a vagrant, or if she was local woman she could be bound over to be of good behaviour. Next to that record, in the same source, was another evocative entry. 'We present – Isabel Holmes being lately brought to bed with a child her husband having been absent for several years.'

The problem was not just one of morals and adultery by Isabel Holmes; it was the involvement of the justices at sessions in dealing with the problems of bastardy. All 18th century quarter sessions records contain references to this subject. Illegitimate children were liable to become a charge on the parish. Establishing the identity of the father enabled orders to be made against him for the maintenance of the child. Disobeying the order would lead the father to prison. In the following year there was another case of prostitution and procurement for the justices.

Berwick-upon-Tweed Quarter Sessions Book 1727 -1745.

Monday 10th November 1730.

Whereas it has been proved to us on the oaths of Barbara Hughes and Esther Buglas that Frances Campbell alias Kerr did entice, delude and draw them respectively into the company of two Serv't Officers within this Borough in order to be by them debauched & Vitiated. It is hereby ordered that the said

Frances Campbell als Kerr be set in the stocks for one hour and that she be bound to the good behaviour for one year next ensuing.

(Northumberland Record Office Access No. C.8/2)

The meagre facts given here suggest that Campbell was drawing impressionable young women into the seamy business of prostitution. If not, there would surely have been a more serious charge and punishment. The stocks at Berwick are said to have stood on the south side of the Town Hall. The town had a set of stocks large enough to seat three offenders side by side and a replica set can be seen outside the Town Hall today. According to the information plaque, the stocks were used as late as 1849 for a woman who failed pay a fine for drunkenness.

There are several examples during the next few years of offenders pleading benefit of clergy, thereby saving their lives, but then being transported in accordance with the Transportation Act. William Johnson, a soldier, in 1733 for example, charged with burglary and stealing 240 guineas, and James Waite in 1740 for stealing iron bars; each man was sentenced to be transported for seven years. Two of the local justices were appointed to arrange a contract for the transportation with a ship's master. Women were not excluded, of course, on 23 May 1739 Isabel Clark, for stealing handkerchiefs value one shilling, was ordered for transportation to America for seven years. Martha Prince was ordered for transportation on 3 March 1745 for seven years for stealing, having first saved her life by pleading benefit of clergy.

James Clarkson was hanged on 19 November 1740 for burglary at the house of George Ord and stealing gold and clothing. He was to be the first person executed at Berwick for nearly 70 years, but, somewhat surprisingly, the justices ordered that the new gallows erected for the occasion should remain up after his execution.

On 18 January 1741/1742, a baker named John Rule was found guilty of two charges of assault with intent to commit gross indecency and was sentenced to stand in the pillory from 11am to 1pm on 23 and 27 January then to be discharged from gaol the following day after payment of fees.

On 3 March 1746 Mary Scott, a spinster of Berwick was tried at the General Gaol Delivery for smothering her baby son. She was sentenced to death, but later pardoned by the King. Two months later, on the 16 June

1746, there was a military execution by firing squad of a Welshman named Lewis and an Irishman named Baillie, both for desertion. On 6 February 1747/48 George Maccan, who had deserted no less than four times (including one time when he joined Bonnie Prince Charlie's rebel forces) and was 'much addicted to stealing', attempted to escape from gaol on the morning of his execution. The noise of the drum beating the reveille covered the noise made by Maccan as he used his handcuffs to beat large pieces of stone out of the wall. When he was discovered, onlookers could scarcely believe that he had done so much damage without the use of a large hammer. Despite his efforts, Maccan was shot.

The next civil execution was on 3 May 1758. Margaret Drydon was hanged for murdering her baby daughter by cutting the child's throat with a knife. It seems likely that all concerned took the view that using a knife required an element of preparation and forethought absent in the case of Mary Scott mentioned above.

The hangman at Margaret Drydon's execution was George Lindsey and his fee was the traditional one, the value of a Scottish Mark, 12 shillings and sixpence (Berwick-upon-Tweed Quarter Sessions Order Books 1758 – 1781 Northumberland Record Office Access No. C.8/4).

At Berwick, as elsewhere, there are examples of women being whipped either privately or through the streets. In July 1762 Alice Hariott was sentenced (for stealing) to be privately whipped by one of the beadles. That punishment would be done in the gaol. In January 1776, Margaret Watson was whipped from the Town Hall to Scotsgate and back again for stealing a chair.

In the records for 1786 there is an example of the jury at the General Gaol Delivery at Berwick returning a guilty verdict against a man for stealing goods valued at less than one shilling. Peter Abel was charged with stealing goods worth 37s 6d but found guilty of stealing goods value tenpence. This demonstrates the reluctance of the jury to return verdicts that would attract the death penalty, that is to say for stealing goods valued at more than one shilling.

Benefit of Clergy was abolished in 1827 and the Berwick records of 1805 reveal what must be one of the last examples of its use. William Chisholm, convicted of several burglaries at Berwick, was asked if he had anything to say before the court passed judgement on him and 'said that he is a clerk and prayeth the benefit of clergy to be allowed him on this behalf (Northumberland Record Office Access No. BRO 262.) He was sentenced to seven years' transportation.

On 3 May 1813 the General Gaol Delivery was again in session. Before them were two highway robbers, soldiers, charged with robbing a man called John Kenton of his watch and a small sum outside Berwick. They were found guilty and sentenced to death, but the jury recommended mercy because of their youth.

According to the *Newcastle Courant* of Saturday 8 May, 1813, 'Much is the credit of the inhabitants of Berwick and the police of the town, the above is the only capital conviction in that borough since 1758.' There had, strictly speaking, been many capital convictions at Berwick since 1758 but no executions. In the borough of Berwick-upon-Tweed the Recorder pronounced the death sentence on a condemned prisoner but it was the coroner who was provided with the death warrant to cause the execution to take place. In all the shire counties and county boroughs in England and Wales that responsibility fell on the High Sheriff and the Town Sheriff respectively. However this proved to be academic as the two men were reprieved and transported.

Death sentences were passed on five offenders at the gaol delivery in 1816: Bernard Duffie and his wife Margaret, James Moen his wife Mary, and Maria Courtney. These people had become involved in the dangerous game of counterfeiting the coin of the realm, which was an act of treason and in the normal course of events would carry the penalty of being hanged drawn and quartered. The court record shows that seven people were tried and five convicted. The convicted counterfeiters were not sentenced to be quartered, but:

> to be taken from hence to the place from whence they came & from thence to be drawn on a hurdle to the Place of Execution and there be hanged by the neck until their bodies be dead.

They were all later reprieved and transported for life.

Six years later the last person to be executed at Berwick-upon-Tweed was tried. She was a woman named Grace Griffin who was accused of the murder of her husband, John Griffin, an unlicensed publican in the town. There were indications that they led a troubled life. Grace Griffin was bound over at the Quarter Sessions in January 1821, what for is not clear. Her husband was also bound over in 1823 in connection with an assault on a woman called Isabella Pearson. Successive witnesses at the trial described a history of heavy drinking by John and Grace Griffin, frequent quarrels and violence between them and a deeply unhappy marriage. In the early hours of the morning, when her husband was helpless through drink, Grace Griffin was alleged to have beaten and stamped on him causing a ruptured bladder and other internal injuries leading to his death. She was found guilty and executed on Saturday 26th July 1823 before an immense crowd. According to the *Newcastle Courant* of Saturday 2 August 1823, 'The wretched sufferer conducted herself with apparent calmness and propriety.'

Appendix 1

Newcastle upon Tyne and Northumberland Assizes

Judges of Assize 1700- 1800

1700	5 August Sir John Turton and Sir John Blencowe
1701	19 August Sir Edward Ward, Lord Chief Baron and Sir John Turton
1702	3 August Thomas Trevor and Littleton Powis
1703	2 August Thomas Trevor and Sir John Blencowe
1704	14 August Sir Edward Ward and Littleton Powis
1705	6 August John Powell and Sir John Blencowe
1706	29 July Sir Edward Ward and Robert Tracey
1707	Sir John Blencowe and Thomas Bury
1708	Robert Tracey and Thomas Bury
1709	Sir Littleton Powis and Thomas Bury
1710	Sir John Powell and Robert Price
1711	30 July Sir Thomas Parker and Sir Thomas Bury
1712	18 August Sir Littleton Powis and Sir Thomas Bury
1713	3 August Sir Thomas Bury and Sir Robert Dormer
1714	2nd August Robert Tracy Esq., and Sir Thomas Powis
1715	22 August Sir Robert Price and Sir James Montague Knight
1716	20 August Sir James Montague and - Hanbury
1717	26 August Robert Dormer Esq and John Fortescue Eland
1718	18 August Sir James Montague and Sir Francis Page
1719	3 August Sir James Montague and Sir Francis Page
1720	15 August Sir James Montague and Sir Francis Page
1721	7 August Mr. Justice Tracy and Mr. Baron Price
1722	24 August Lord Chief Justice King and Mr. Baron Gilbert
1723	
1724	23 August Sir Francis Page and Sir Alexander Denton
1725	2 August Robert Price and James Reynold Esqrs.
1726	8 August Sir Francis Page and Sir Bernard Hall
1727	7 August Sir Edmund Probin and Sir Laurence Carter
1728	19 August Sir John Cummyns and Spencer Cowper Esq.
1729	4 August Sir Francis Page and Sir Bernard Hall
1730	20 July Sir Francis Page and Sir John Fortescue
1731	16 August Sir Alexander Denton and Sir Edmund Probyn

1732	31 July Sir Francis Page and Sir William Thompson
1733	6 August Sir Robert Eyre and Thomas Reeve Esq.
1734	5 August Sir Francis Page and Thomas Reeve Esq.
1735	28 July Sir Alexander Denton and Mr. Justice Lee
1736	16 August Mr Justice Lee and Mr. Baron Fortescue
1737	8 August Mr Baron Fortescue and Sir William Chapple
1738	31 July William Fortescue Esq. and Sir William Chapple
1739	20 August Sir William Chapple and Mr. Baron Parker
1740	4 August Thomas Parker and James Reynolds
1741	28 July Thomas Parker and Martin Wright
1742	17 August Thomas Burnit and Samuel Urlin
1743	2 August Thomas Dennison and John Birch
1744	23 July Thomas Burnitt and Charles Clarke
1745	12 August Edward Clive and John Bird
1746	4 August Sir Thomas Parker and Thomas Burnitt
1747	17 August John Birch and Sir Heneage Legge
1748	6 August Sir Edward Clive and Sir Heneage Legge
1749	27 July Sir Thomas Abney and Thomas Dennison
1750	13 August Edward Clive and Sydney Stafford Smyth
1751	5 August John Birch and Sir Heneage Legge
1752	27 July John Birch and Sir Heneage Legge
1753	21 August Sir Heneage Legge and Eyre
1754	12 August Sir Heneage Legge and Sydney Stafford Smyth
1755	29 July Sir Richard Adams and Henry Bathurst
1756	25 August Henry Bathurst and Sir John Eardley Wilmot
1757	8 August Henry Bathurst and William Noel
1758	24 July Lord Chief Justice Mansfield and Sydney Stafford Smyth
1759	13 August Henry Bathurst and William Noel
1760	4 August Henry Bathurst and Sir Richard Lloyd
1761	28 July Henry Bathurst and Sir Richard Lloyd
1762	7 August Henry Bathurst and Sir Henry Gould
1763	7 August Sir Henry Gould and George Parrot
1764	20 August Henry Bathurst and Sir Joseph Yates
1765	5 August Sir Henry Gould and Sir Joseph Yates
1766	26 July Henry Bathurst and George Parrot
1767	17 August Sir Henry Gould and George Parrot
1768	5 August Sir Henry Gould and Sir Joseph Yates
1769	24 July Sir Henry Gould and George Parrot

1770	20 August The Hon. George Parrot and Sir Richard Aston
1771	7 July Sir Henry Gould and the Hon. Edward Willes.
1772	15 August Sir Henry Gould and the Hon. Edward Willes.
1773	7 August Sir Henry Gould and Sir William Blackstone.
1774	30 July Sir Henry Gould and Sir William Blackstone
1775	12 August Sir Henry Gould and Sir William Henry Ashurst.
1776	3 August Sir Henry Gould and Sir William Henry Ashurst
1777	26 July Sir Henry Gould and Sir George Nares.
1778	15 August The Hon. Edward Willes and Sir Beaumont Hotham.
1779	31 July The Hon Edward Willes and Sir Francis Buller.
1780	12 August Lord Loughborough and Sir Beaumont Hotham
1781	11 August Sir George Nares and the Hon. John Heath
1782	27 July Lord Chief Baron Skinner and Baron Eyre
1783	16 August Sir James Eyre and the Hon. Francis Buller.
1784	9 August Baron Perryn and Justice John Heath
1785	25 July Sir George Nares and Justice John Heath
1786	14 August Hon Francis Buller and Justice John Heath
1787	13 August Lord Loughborough and Judge John Wilson
1788	21 July Justice Nathaniel Grose and Baron Alexander Thompson
1789	10 August Sir John Wilson and the Hon Baron Alexander Thompson
1790	6 August Sir John Wilson and the Hon Baron Alexander Thompson
1791	22 August Sir Nathaniel Grose and Baron Alexander Thompson.
1792	6 August Lord Kenyon and Baron Alexander Thompson.
1793	29 July Chief Baron Archibald Macdonald and Baron Thompson
1794	18 August Sir Giles Rooke and Sir Soulden Lawrence.
1795	3 August Sir Giles Rooke and Sir Soulden Lawrence.
1796	25 July Sir Giles Rooke and Sir Soulden Lawrence.
1797	14 August Baron Thompson and Sir Giles Rooke.
1798	6 August Sir Giles Rooke and Sir Soulden Lawrence
1799	22 July Sir Soulden Lawrence and Sir Sim. Le Blanc
1800	11 August Sir Allan Chambre and the Hon. Robert Graham.

Appendix 2

Deaths of prisoners in the Morpeth Gaol (Morpeth Parish Records)

1679	13 May	Christopher RIDLEY a Prissoner out of ye Jaile.
1687	3 July	Mr. Joshua WETWANGG dyed in ye Jaile and buried in ye Quire of Morpeth
1717	31 May	Isaac COOPER died in gaol
1718	14 Nov.	Mr Thomas SHAFTO died in gaol
1724	17 July	Nicholas HEDLEY died in gaol
1725/6, 5 March		Thomas SMITH a prisoner
1727	8 April	John DUNN, Died in Gaol
1727	12 Sept.	(BLANK), in gaol
1727	20 Nov.	John WALTON a prisoner in the gaol
1727/8 25 Feb.		Nicholas ROBSON, in gaol
1728/9 26 March		Elizabeth PURDY in gaol
1728	30 June	William CHARLTON in ye gaol
1731	19 Dec.	William GLADSTONE died in gaol
1731/2 13 Jan.		William WALTON a prisoner
1735	24 April	Gawin DAVISON of Aidon Bridge, prisoner in ye gaol, charity
1736	25 August	John SCOWGOLD died in gaol
1738/9 16 Feb.		Elizabeth NIXON from the Correction House
1740	12 Dec.	John MACKNAB from the Correction House
1741	15 May	John BELL out of the gaol
1741	5 May	Bartholomew READHEAD out of the gaol
1741	13 June	James HARVEY out of the gaol
1741	23 Jan.	Elinor HEWISON out of the Correction House
1741/2 14 March		John WILSON out of the Correction House
1742	24 April	Mr William JOHNSON, a clergyman, out of the gaol, charity
1742	23 June	William WAITE, charity, out of the gaol
1745	27 May	Jane daughter to Richard CHAPMAN, a Fellon in the Gaol, charity
1746	9 April	Adam THOMPSON, out of the gaol, charity
1746	19 April	John BELL out of the gaol, charity

1746	17 July	Thomas STEWART, out of the gaol, charity
1751	1 March	Thomas ARMSTRONG, a prisoner
		In Morpeth Gaol, charity
1773	9 March	William MILLER, from ye gaol
1775	1 Nov.	Charles QUEENBY from ye gaol
1776	17 April	Ann BROWN, from ye gaol
1776	1 May	Joseph PIGG out of ye gaol
1776	10 May	William CUNNINGHAM, from ye gaol
1779	22 May	James PARSON from ye gaol
1782	21 Jan.	George WRIGHT from ye gaol
1786	18 August	Charles HALL from ye gaol
1788	7 June	Lionel Forster

An old drawing of Morpeth gaol.

Suggested reading

Histories

History of Northumberland by John Hodgson 1835
History of Northumberland, 15 volumes 1890 – 1940, various editors, Northumberland County History Committee
History of Morpeth, John Hodgson, 1832
History of Berwick-upon-Tweed, James Fuller 1799
Berwick-upon-Tweed, the History of the Town and Guild, John Scott, 1888
A Place by Itself, Berwick-upon-Tweed in the 18th century, David Brenchley 1997

Prisons

The State of the Prisons in England and Wales by John Howard, 1776-1792
A History of English Prison Administration 1750-1877 by Sean McConville, Routledge, Keegan and Paul, 1981
The Fabrication of Virtue; English Prison Architecture 1750-1840 by Robin Evans, Cambridge UP 1982

Punishments

Bygone Punishments by William Andrews 1899
Of Bridles and Burnings, The Punishment of Women by E.J. Burford and Sandra Shulman, Hale 1992

Transportation of convicts

Convicts and the Colonies by A.G.L. Shaw, Faber and Faber 1966
The Fatal Shore by Robert Hughes, Collins Harvill, 1987
The Search for John Small – First Fleeter by Mollie Gillen, Library of Australian History, Sydney, 1988
The Complete Book of Emigrants in Bondage 1614-1775 by Peter Wilson Coldham Genealogical Pub. Corp. Baltimore, 1988
Emigrants in Chains by Peter Wilson Coldham, Allan Smith, 1992
The Slave Trade, The History of the Atlantic Slave Trade 1440-1870 by Hugh Thomas, Picador 1997

Crime in the Eighteenth Century

The London Hanged by Peter Linebaugh, Allen Lane, Penguin Press 1991
The Hanging Tree by V.C.A. Gatrell, Oxford UP 1994
The Thieves Opera by Lucy Moore, Penguin 1998
Rogues, Thieves and the Rule of Law by Gwenda Morgan and Peter Rushton, UCL Press 1998

Life in the Eighteenth Century

England in the Eighteenth Century by P.H. Plumb, Pelican 1950
London Life in the Eighteenth Century by M Dorothy George, Penguin 1966
Tyneside newspapers, Central Library, Newcastle upon Tyne

A note on the Julian and Gregorian Calendars

The calendar in use in Great Britain up to 1752 was the old Julian Calendar. The year began on 25 March and ended the following 24 March, so January, February and most of March came at the end of the year not the beginning. Centuries of experience had shown that the Julian Calendar was not correctly lined up with the equinoxes and in 1582 countries elsewhere in Europe adopted the Gregorian Calendar we use today. There could be confusion about the year for the months of January, February and March and in the early 1700s the practice sprang up in public records and newspapers, for example, of expressing the dates in the manner of both calendars. 14 January 1720/1721 for example indicated the year was 1720 by the Julian Calendar, but 1721 under the Gregorian Calendar. This confusing system was resolved and abandoned in 1752 when Great Britain adopted the Gregorian Calendar and lined up with Europe by dropping 11 days from the 3 to 13 of September 1752 inclusive and 1 January was declared henceforth to be New Years Day.

Select index of persons mentioned in the text